S0-DMP-700

Electrical Connections

Authors

Maureen Allen	Judie Kirkhart
Diane Bredt	Howard Larimer
Judy Calderwood	Sheryl Mercier
Peter Chambers	Sandy Schmeling
Debby Deal	Vincent Sipkovich
Evalyn Hoover	Mike Walsh
Gale Phillips Kahn	

Illustrators

Max Cantu	Brenda Howsepian	Sheryl Mercier

Editors

Gretchen Winkleman	Dave Youngs

AIMS Education Foundation • Fresno, California

This book contains materials developed by the AIMS Education Foundation in cooperation with the Fresno Unified School District and the Irvine (California) Unified School District. **AIMS** (**A**ctivities **I**ntegrating **M**athematics and **S**cience) was begun in 1981 with a grant from the National Science Foundation. The non-profit AIMS Education Foundation publishes hands-on instructional materials (books and the monthly AIMS Newsletter) that integrate curricular disciplines such as mathematics, science, language arts, and social studies. The Foundation sponsors a national program of professional development through which educators may gain both an understanding of the AIMS philosophy and expertise in teaching by integrated, hands-on methods.

ISBN 1-881431-28-2

Printed in the United States of America

Table of Contents

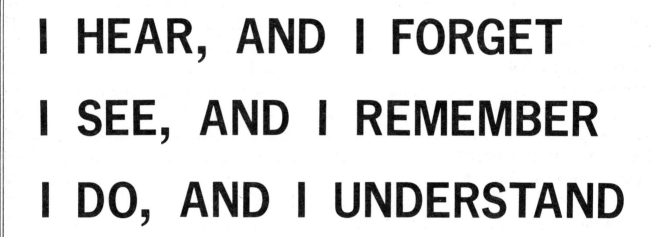

I HEAR, AND I FORGET

I SEE, AND I REMEMBER

I DO, AND I UNDERSTAND

—Chinese Proverb

Conceptual Overview

Electrical Connections was written to provide hands-on activities for students in grades four through nine. Electricity is often viewed as something mysterious, and perhaps even dangerous, by young and old alike. This book is an attempt to help clear up some of the mystery and alleviate some of the fear by learning a few basic electrical concepts. Since it is such an integral part of our modern world, it is imperative that students learn about electricity.

The following is a list of the major concepts covered in this book:

• Atoms are the basic building blocks of nature. Atoms, in turn, are composed of smaller particles called electrons, protons, and neutrons. Electrons and protons have a property called charge. Electrons have a negative charge, while protons have a positive charge.

• Static electricity occurs when electrons (negative charges) are transferred from one object to another through friction. Objects that gain extra electrons have a net negative charge. Objects that lose electrons have a positive charge. Most objects have approximately the same number of protons and electrons and have no net electrical charge.

• Like electric charges repel one another. Unlike charges attract.

• Materials are classified according to how well they conduct electricity. Conductors readily carry an electric current. Semiconductors conduct electricity to a lesser degree. Insulators do not normally conduct electricity.

• In order for an electric current to flow, it must have an uninterrupted conducting path. An electric circuit is such a path.

• There are two basis types of circuits; series and parallel. In a series circuit, the current has only one path; any break in that path will interrupt the flow of electricity. In a parallel circuit there are multiple paths for the current; a break in one path will not interrupt the flow of electricity in the other paths.

• Electric switches are placed in circuits to start and stop the flow of electricity.

• There is a direct connection between electricity and magnetism. They are both part of the fundamental electromagnetic force. An electric current produces a magnetic field. A moving magnetic field can create an electric current.

Math Content	Estimating	Measuring	Recording data	Computing	Problem solving	Writing formulas	Sequencing	Graphing	Venn diagrams	Patterning
Atoms										
Static Strokes	✔	✔	✔							
Different Strokes		✔	✔							
Balance Your Charge Account				✔						
Nature's Light and Sound Show		✔		✔	✔	✔	✔			
Sparky's Light Kit					✔					
Path Finders								✔		
Circuit Quiz Boards							✔			
Wet Cell Battery										
Conductor or Insulator?									✔	
Make a Dimmer Switch		✔					✔			
Make a Switch										
Circuit Breakers										
Electric Circuits										
Short Cuts										
Put Your Name in Lights					✔					✔
Electromagnetic Connection										
Make a Galvanometer										
How to Make an Electric Motor										
Electromagnets	✔	✔	✔	✔	✔	✔	✔	✔		✔
Electricity Time Line	✔	✔					✔			
When I Was Ten				✔			✔			

Science Processing Skills

	Observing	Making & testing hypotheses	Classifying	Drawing conclusions	Controlling Variables	Collecting data	Organizing data	Recording data
Atoms			✔					
Static Strokes	✔	✔	✔	✔				
Different Strokes			✔	✔	✔			
Balance Your Charge Account		✔						
Nature's Light and Sound Show	✔	✔		✔		✔		
Sparky's Light Kit	✔	✔		✔				
Path Finders	✔	✔		✔		✔	✔	
Circuit Quiz Boards	✔					✔	✔	✔
Wet Cell Battery	✔	✔		✔				
Conductor or Insulator?	✔	✔		✔				
Make a Dimmer Switch	✔	✔		✔				
Make a Switch	✔	✔		✔				
Circuit Breakers	✔	✔		✔				
Electric Circuits	✔	✔		✔				
Short Cuts	✔	✔		✔				
Put Your Name in Lights	✔		✔					
Electromagnetic Connection	✔	✔		✔				
Make a Galvanometer	✔			✔				
How to Make an Electric Motor	✔			✔	✔			
Electromagnets	✔	✔	✔	✔	✔	✔	✔	✔
Electricity Time Line			✔			✔	✔	
When I Was Ten			✔			✔		✔

Dear family,

Soon our class will study electricity. We will be doing many experiments to help us understand things like bulbs, batteries, circuits, and switches. These activities will require a variety of materials. If you would like to lend or donate any of the materials listed below, please send them to school by _____.

Thank you,

_____
    student

_____
    teacher

batteries (all sizes)   wire strippers (mark with name)

flashlight bulbs   aluminum foil

electrical wire   miniature Christmas tree lights
                                  (will be cut up)

ELECTRICAL EQUIPMENT ALTERNATIVES

1 WIRE  bell wire (20 gauge)   or   aluminum foil strips, backed or covered with masking tape

2 BULB flashlight bulbs   or   miniature Christmas lights (replace bulb and holder)

cut lights apart

3 BULB HOLDER or   clamp   foil strip clamped next to the side of the bulb

or

 tape wire to side of bulb

tape wire to end of bulb

4 SWITCH  or   2 brass paper fasteners
1 piece of tagboard
1 large paper clip

 **Poster Contest**

Choose one of these topics or make up your own:

- A safe home is a happy home!
- Stay away from fallen wires.
- Keep the radio away from the bath tub!
- I'm smart! I check for worn cords.
- Use the right size fuse.

Rules:

Posters must be finished by _____.

Atoms

Topic Area
Atomic structure

Introductory Statement
Students will make simple models of atoms.

Materials
Per set of atoms:
 construction paper
 plastic bag of miniature marshmallows, 10 each of 3
  different colors
 glue
 markers

Key Question
How can we make a model of an atom that shows its electrons, protons, and neutrons?

Background Information
All matter is made up of atoms, which in turn are made up of smaller particles called *protons, neutrons,* and *electrons.* Together, protons and neutrons form the central core, or *nucleus,* of an atom. Electrons, which have only 1/1840 the mass of protons and neutrons, orbit the nucleus in layers called *shells.*

There are rules by which the shells operate. In the innermost shell near the nucleus, only two electrons can orbit. In the second shell, only eight can orbit. Other shells beyond this can hold more electrons, except for the outermost shell, which never has more than eight.

There are 92 naturally occurring kinds of atoms found on earth, each with a different number of protons, electrons, and neutrons. The number of electrons in the outermost shell determines the chemical properties of the atom. Each different kind of atom is called an *element* and is identified by its *atomic number* (the number of protons in the atom). Chemists also define an element as a simple substance that cannot be broken down into any smaller component by ordinary chemical reactions.

Protons and electrons have a property called *charge.* All electric phenomena are caused by charges. By convention, protons are said to have a positive charge and electrons a negative charge. Neutrons have no charge. Most atoms have the same number of protons and electrons and are electrically balanced. If an atom has different numbers of protons and electrons, it is called an *ion.* If there are more electrons than protons, it is a negative ion. If there are more protons than electrons, it is a positive ion.

It is impossible to picture atoms accurately; for example, electrons have a dual nature and can take the form of both particles and waves. The only accurate model of an atom is an abstract, mathematical one. Since this type of model does not help most people understand atoms, several other models are usually used when describing atoms. The most common is the Bohr model. It pictures a central mass (nucleus) made up of protons and neutrons orbited by electrons.

The Bohr model, like all non-mathematical ones, has distortions of the size and space relationships within an atom. It is difficult to accurately convey the vastness of the empty space within atoms. If an atom were two miles in diameter, it would appear to be solid, since the electrons would be orbiting the outer shell at almost the speed of light. Yet, its nucleus would only be about the size of a golf ball and its electrons the size of BB's; all the rest would be empty space.

The atom model used in this lesson is similar to the Bohr model. While not very accurate, it does show the basic parts of an atom and the atomic shells. It is intended to be a starting point for students in building their conceptualization of the atom.

Management
1. Students can work alone or in groups.
2. Plastic bags with the marshmallows should be made up ahead of time for individuals or groups.
3. Three colors of colored dots, colored cereal, or construction paper circles can be used instead of marshmallows to represent the protons, electrons, and neutrons.
4. Since electrons are so much smaller than protons and neutrons, smaller bits of marshmallow, or smaller colored dots can be used to represent them.
5. The activity sheet can be used to make models of atoms if the other materials are not available.

Procedure
1. Students will make models of three different atoms. Draw a diagram of an atom on the board and tell the students that atoms are made up of three important parts: protons, neutrons, and electrons. You may want to tell students about the charges on protons (+) and electrons (-).
2. Explain that atoms are the building blocks of matter and that they differ only in the number of protons, electrons, and neutrons. Tell students that the number of protons present (the atomic number) determines what type of atom it will be. For example, carbon has an atomic number of 6. It has 6 protons, 6 electrons, and usually 6 neutrons.
3. Demonstrate how to make a model of an atom. Using three different colors of marshmallows and a piece of

construction paper, construct a model of a helium atom. Glue two "protons" (first color of marshmallows) and two "neutrons" (second color) together in the center of the "atom" to form the nucleus. Draw a circle (shell) around this nucleus and glue two "electrons" (third color) somewhere on the circle. Since the mass of the electrons is much less than the mass of the protons and neutrons, use small pieces of marshmallow to represent each electron.

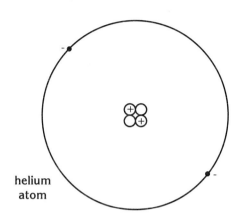

helium
atom

4. Pass out the marshmallows and construction paper. Have students construct a hydrogen atom (1 proton, 1 electron), a helium atom (2 protons, 2 neutrons, 2 electrons), and a carbon atom (6 protons, 6 neutrons, 6 electrons). The model of the carbon atom will need two circles (shells). The first shell (inner circle) of the carbon atom has 2 electrons, the second shell (outer circle) has 4 electrons.

5. Students may use markers to draw the electron shells. Markers can also be used to put a (+) on each proton and a (-) on each electron.

6. Students use the remaining three marshmallows to make a key for each atom model (there will be one extra "neutron" left over). For example: pink = proton (+), green = neutron, yellow = electron (-).

7. Discuss the fact that these marshmallow models are only like real atoms in a few ways (they show the three main particles in atoms, they show the nucleus made of protons and electrons, they show the electrons as orbiting the nucleus in shells, they show that electrons and protons have charge). Explain that models sometimes help us understand difficult concepts. Emphasize the fact that real atoms are incredibly small and wondrous things with many amazing properties.

Discussion

1. How are all atoms the same? [made of electrons, protons, and neutrons]

2. What is at the center of every atom? [the nucleus, which is made of protons and neutrons]

3. What orbits the nucleus? [electrons]

4. How is the nucleus of the hydrogen atom different from the nucleus of the helium atom? [The hydrogen atom does not have any neutrons in its nucleus.]

5. How is the carbon atom different from the helium atom? [It has electrons orbiting in two electron shells.]

6. What atomic particle is related to the word electricity? [electron]

7. How could we build models of other atoms? [Use different numbers of marshmallows.]

Extensions

1. Use the activity sheet to make a model of an oxygen atom (atomic number is 8).

2. Make models of other atoms. You will need more than two shells for larger atoms.

3. Use other materials to make models of atoms.

4. Study the periodic table. Look at how the number of electrons in the outer shell of an atom determines what family it is in.

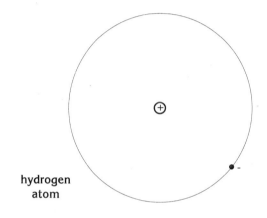

hydrogen
atom

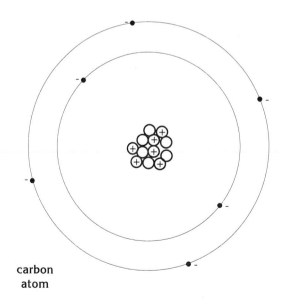

carbon
atom

AT MS

atom's name

_____

protons

neutrons

electrons

3

Static Electricity

Have you ever rubbed a balloon on your hair and then stuck the balloon to the wall? Static electricity was at work!

All matter is made up of tiny particles called atoms.
Each atom contains 3 basic parts:

    protons which have a positive electrical charge (+)
    electrons which have a negative electrical charge (-)
    neutrons which have no electrical charge

Protons and neutrons are in the *nucleus* or central core of an atom, while the electrons orbit around the nucleus.

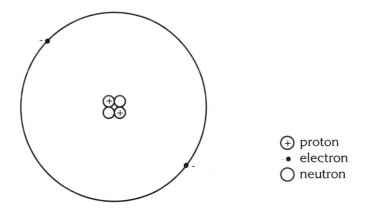

⊕ proton
· electron
◯ neutron

Most objects, such as a balloon, normally have about the same number of electrons and protons, making them electrically balanced.

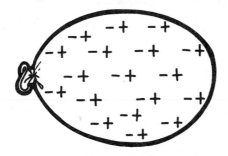

Sometimes objects gain or lose electrons through *friction* (rubbing 2 things together). When this happens the object becomes electrically charged. If an object gains electrons when it is rubbed, it becomes negatively charged because it has more electrons (-) than protons (+). If an object loses electrons when it is rubbed, it becomes positively charged because it has more protons (+) than electrons (-).

A fundamental principle of electric charges is that like charges repel and unlike charges attract.

When the balloon is rubbed on your hair it gains electrons from your hair and becomes negatively charged. Your hair becomes positively charged and will stick up because like charges repel. When the negatively charged balloon is brought near your hair, it will be attracted because unlike charges attract.

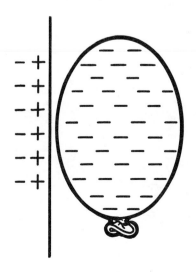

When the negatively charged balloon is brought near a wall, it *induces* a positive charge near the surface of the wall (the extra electrons on the balloon repel electrons near the surface of the wall). Since opposite charges attract, the balloon sticks to the wall.

Static Strokes

Topic Area
Static electricity

Introductory Statement
Students will explore static electricity.

Math
Estimating
Measurement
Recording data

Science
Observing
Predicting
Classifying
Generalizing

Materials
plastic wrap - see *Management Suggestions*
paper towels
variety of small objects to be tested: paper clips, salt, small pieces of aluminum foil, styrofoam pieces, cotton thread

Key Question
How does a statically charged object affect other objects?

Background Information
All objects are composed of atoms which contain positive (produced by protons) and negative (produced by electrons) electric charges. Most objects have no net electric charge and are electrically balanced because they have approximately the same number of electrons as protons. Static electricity occurs when objects become unbalanced electrically. Some materials easily lose or gain electrons, causing them to have, respectively, a net positive or negative charge. When certain materials are rubbed together (e.g., your shoes on a carpet or the plastic wrap and paper towels in this activity), friction causes electrons to be transferred from one material to the other, producing the unbalanced charges we experience as static electricity.

A key property of electricity is that like charges repel each other, while opposite charges attract. Statically charged objects can produce static charges in other objects. For example, a negatively charged balloon sticks to a wall because its negative charge repels electrons in the atoms at the wall's surface (causing them to become polarized), thus inducing a positive charge. Static electricity is most easily observed on cool, dry days when conditions keep the charges from dispersing easily.

Management
1. Have students work in groups of three or four.
2. This activity works best on cool, dry days or inside air-conditioned classrooms.
3. Not all plastic wraps are equal in their static ability. We have found that Reynolds® PLASTIC WRAP, with "BEST CLING" marked on the box, works best.
4. If you don't want to use plastic wrap for *Part 2*, inflated balloons work well. Charge them by rubbing them on clothes or hair.

Procedure
Part 1
1. Pass out plastic wrap and paper towels.
2. Students charge the plastic wrap by placing it flat on a desk and rubbing it with a paper towel. Students lift the plastic wrap from the desk by one corner and observe what happens (it will initially cling to the desk and when lifted will cling to their hands or other nearby objects). Students record their observations.
3. Students charge the plastic wrap again and pick it up by the midpoints of two opposite sides (see illustration). Students observe what happens (the plastic wrap will make a tent shape since the opposite sides have the same charge and repel each other) and record their observations.
4. Discuss what happened in each case.
5. Explain that static electricity is responsible for the phenomena they observed.

Part 2
1. Pass out objects to be tested.
2. Discuss the *Key Question*, "How does a statically charged object affect other objects?"
3. Students work with one set of objects at a time. Students predict what will happen when the charged plastic wrap is held above the objects. After recording predictions in the blank provided, students charge plastic wrap. Two students lift the plastic wrap by the four corners and slowly lower it until it is six to ten cm above the objects. Observe what happens and record observations.
4. The last four objects to be tested should be chosen by the students. Some suggested objects are pencil shavings, erasers, eraser rubbings, iron filings, pieces of thread, bits of tissue, and plastic chips.
5. Discuss the results.
6. Have students fill in the bottom of the sheet.

Discussion
1. Why did the plastic wrap stick to the table and other objects when rubbed with a paper towel? [It picked up electrons from the towel, gaining a net negative charge. This negative charge induced a positive charge in objects near it. These opposite charges produced an attractive force, since unlike charges attract.]
2. Why did the plastic wrap make a tent shape when held by the midpoints of opposite sides? [The net negative charge on the plastic wrap caused the two sides to repel each other, since like charges repel.]
3. Why did the charged plastic wrap pick up some objects, but not others? [The attractive force caused by the static electricity was enough to overcome the force of gravity for the lighter objects, but not the heavier ones.]

Extensions
1. Have students move their fingers close above the surface of the charged plastic wrap as it is attracting bits of styrofoam or other objects. They will be fascinated by the results.
2. Challenge the students to see if they can make some of the objects "dance." This is easy to do with styrofoam bits or small cotton thread.
3. Repeat *Part 2* using balloons instead of plastic wrap.
4. Make "magic wands" by rubbing plastic straws or pens with a paper towel. They will attract light objects. Note: not all types of plastic works well for this.
5. Read about Benjamin Franklin and his experiments with static electricity.

6

STATIC STROKES

Part 1

Place a piece of plastic wrap flat on your desk and rub it with a paper towel. Pick the plastic wrap up by one corner.

What happens? _____

_____

Place the plastic wrap on your desk and rub it with a paper towel again. Pick the plastic wrap up by the midpoints of two opposite sides.

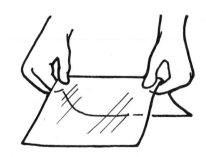

What happens? _____

_____

7

STATIC STROKES

Name _____

Part 2

How does a statically charged object affect other objects?

Charge the plastic wrap. Predict what will happen when it is held 6-10 cm from the following objects. Record your predictions. Hold the plastic wrap flat above the objects listed. Record your observations.

Objects	Predictions	Observations
paper clips		
styrofoam		
small pieces of aluminum foil		
cotton thread		
salt		

I learned that _____

_____

_____

8

Different Strokes

Topic Area
Static electricity

Introductory Statement
Students will experiment with static electricity and discover some of its properties.

Math
Measuring length
Classifying

Science
Observing
Controlling variables
Recording data
Drawing conclusions

Materials
Per group:
2 balloons
piece of nylon material or paper towel
2 30 cm pieces of thread
small bits of paper
book
pencil and pencil shavings
piece of plastic wrap
plastic ruler
tape

Key Questions
Part 1: How does a statically charged object affect other objects?
Part 2: How do balloons with like and unlike charges interact with each other and with other materials?

Background Information
Some materials develop static charges when they are rubbed together. This happens because there is a transfer of electrons (negative charges) from one material to another. The material that gains electrons becomes negatively charged, while the material that loses electrons becomes positively charged. For example, a rubber balloon rubbed by a piece of nylon picks up electrons and becomes negatively charged while the nylon loses electrons and becomes positively charged.

When any two substances listed below are rubbed together, the substance *higher* on the list (which is called the triboelectric or electrostatic series) will become positively charged, while the *lower* one will become negatively charged. The farther apart the two substances are on the list, the greater the charge produced. In each case, the material higher on the list *gives up* electrons (negative charges) to become positively charged, while the other material *receives* extra electrons and becomes negatively charged.

<u>Positive Charge</u> (gives up electrons)
glass
nylon
wool
silk
paper
wood
sealing wax
styrofoam
rubber
plastic wrap
<u>Negative Charge</u> (gains electrons)

If two balloons are rubbed with the same material, they will both have the same charge. Since like charges repel, the balloons will repel each other and not touch. If certain objects are placed between two similarly charged balloons, an opposite charge is induced in the objects and both balloons are attracted to the object. Other objects do not become charged by induction when placed between two similarly charged balloons and the balloons continue to repel each other.

When two balloons are rubbed with different materials, the type and strength of their charges will differ, depending on factors such as their position in the triboelectric series. For example, when one balloon is rubbed with nylon and another is rubbed with plastic wrap, they will have opposite charges and will attract each other. This happens because opposite charges attract.

For more information see *Static Strokes*.

Management
1. The static electricity lessons are best done on cool, dry days. Warm, moist air will conduct electric charges away from an object as soon as they are formed. An invisible coat of moisture on materials permits the electric charges to run off into the area surrounding the object.
2. Gather all materials for the activity and place them in a basket or box for each group.
3. Students can use their hair to charge the balloons instead of nylon or paper towels. Their hair should be clean and dry.
4. Not all plastic wraps are equal in their static ability. We have found that Reynolds® PLASTIC WRAP, with "BEST CLING" marked on the box, works best.

Procedure
Part 1
1. Ask the *Key Question*: "How does a statically charged object affect other objects?"

2. Rub a balloon with a piece of nylon or paper towel and touch the balloon to a wall. Discuss what happens and why. [It has become negatively charged and induces a positive charge near the surface of the wall. Since opposite charges attract, it sticks to the wall because of the electrostatic forces.]
3. Tell students that they will be observing the effects that a charged balloon has on different objects. Have students do the tasks as they are presented on the activity sheet.
4. Discuss the results as a class. Have students write their conclusions in the space provided at the bottom of the activity sheet.

Part 2
1. Have students blow up their second balloons. Tie each balloon to a 30 cm piece of thread.
2. Students tape the balloons to the edge of a table so that there is a three to five cm space between the balloons.
3. Students charge one balloon by rubbing it with a piece of plastic wrap (giving it a positive charge) and the other by rubbing it with a piece of nylon (giving it a negative charge). Have students observe the effects of the unlike charges and record what happens on the activity sheet.
4. Students charge both balloons with a piece of nylon, giving them both a negative charge. Have them observe the effects of like charges on the two balloons and record what happens on the activity sheet.
5. Students charge both balloons by rubbing them with a piece of nylon and then hold their hands, plastic rulers, papers, and plastic wrap between the two balloons. Observe and record what happens. Encourage students to try other materials and observe the results.
6. Discuss the results as a class, and have students write their conclusions in the space provided at the bottom of the activity sheet.

Discussion
1. Allow each group to share the results of one of the activities and explain why they think it happened the way it did.
2. Ask students if they think there would be a difference in the results if it was a rainy day.
3. What happens when a statically charged balloon is brought near light objects?
4. What happens when a statically charged balloon is brought near heavy objects?
5. How do the two balloons interact when they have opposite charges?
6. How do the two balloons interact when they have the same charge?
7. What happens when an object is placed between the balloons with like charges? Does the type of object make a difference?

Extensions
1. Use styrofoam cups instead of balloons and test the results.
2. Repeat *Part 2* using positively charged balloons.
3. Ask students to conduct their own static electricity experiments and share the results with the class.

Curriculum Correlations
Language arts: Read the story, *The Red Balloon*. Read a book about Benjamin Franklin. A good one is the story *Ben and Me*.
Art: Students can draw faces on the balloons with markers or use static electricity to stick on pieces of yarn, paper, etc. for the features.

Different Strokes

Part 1

How does a statically charged balloon affect other objects?

Blow up a balloon and knot the end. Charge the balloon by rubbing it with a piece of nylon. Complete each test below and mark the statement that describes the result.

Test		
Bring a charged balloon near small pieces of paper. Observe what happens.	affects paper	no effect on paper
Bring a charged balloon near a piece of thread. Observe what happens.	affects thread	no effect on thread
Bring a charged balloon near a pencil. Observe what happens.	affects pencil	no effect on pencil
Bring a charged balloon near somebody's hair. Observe what happens.	affects hair	no effect on hair
Bring a charged balloon near a book. Observe what happens.	affects book	no effect on book
Bring a charged balloon near some pencil shavings. Observe what happens.	affects shavings	no effect on shavings

Conclusions: _____

_____

_____

Part 2

Blow up a second balloon. Use two pieces of thread and tape to hang both balloons from the edge of a table so they are 3-5 cm apart.

Charge one balloon with a piece of plastic wrap and the other with nylon. Observe the interaction.	opposite charges attract	opposite charges repel	no effect
Charge both balloons by rubbing with a piece of nylon. Observe the interaction.	like charges attract	like charges repel	no effect
Charge both balloons by rubbing with a piece of nylon. Hold your hand between the balloons. Does the interaction between the balloons change?		interaction affected by hand	interaction not affected
Charge both balloons with nylon. Hold a plastic ruler between them. Does the interaction between the balloons change?		interaction affected by ruler	interaction not affected
Charge both balloons with nylon. Hold a piece of paper between them. Does the interaction between the balloons change?		interaction affected by paper	interaction not affected
Charge both balloons with nylon. Hold a piece of plastic wrap between them. Does the interaction between the balloons change?		interaction affected by wrap	interaction not affected

Conclusions: _____

_____

_____

St. Elmo's Fire

Many years ago, when sailing ships traveled at night, sailors were sometimes frightened by a strange, bluish light dancing on the masts of their ships. The light was often accompanied by crackling noises. They named the effect St. Elmo's Fire after the patron saint of sailors.

In the years since, St. Elmo's Fire has become the unwanted companion of aviators as well. Airplane pilots sometimes see St. Elmo's Fire when they fly near thunderstorms or cumulonimbus clouds. The light appears on the wings and propellers of airplanes, ships' masts, and other objects that are higher than their surroundings.

St. Elmo's Fire, or corona discharge, is not a fire at all. It is really a discharge of static electricity. Static electricity is called that to distinguish it from current electricity; static electricity remains stationary until it builds up enough electric potential to discharge, while the more familiar current electricity moves through electrical circuits in a steady, predictable manner. Static electricity often builds up on tall objects when the atmosphere is full of electrical charges. That is why St. Elmo's Fire is most often seen and heard before or during a thunderstorm.

Static electricity can produce shocks, St. Elmo's Fire, lightning, and other serious problems. In 1937, static electricity may have sparked the explosion of the hydrogen-filled airship Hindenburg as it was docking at Lakehurst, New Jersey.

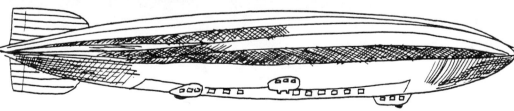

The Hindenburg
length: 245 meters (804 feet)
width: 41 meters (135 feet)
volume: 199,980 cubic meters (7,062,100 cubic feet)
cruising speed: 126 kilometers (78 miles) per hour

Balance Your Charge Account

Topic Area
Static electricity

Introductory Statement
Students play a game reinforcing static electricity concepts.

Materials
For each group:
  game board
  1 paper fastener
  1 paper clip
  small objects of different colors (buttons or plastic chips) to use as game pieces - (1 per person)
  crayons or markers
For each student:
  scissors

Background Information
This game reviews some of the ways that static electric charges can be produced on a balloon. When the game begins, the balloon is electrically balanced, since it has the same number of positive and negative charges. As the game is played, negative charges are gained and lost. If there are more negative charges than positive ones on the balloon, it has a negative charge. If there are more positive charges than negative, the balloon has a positive charge.

Management
1. This game provides a good review of static electric concepts. It should be played after students have done several hands-on activities with static electricity.
2. The game boards should be made ahead of time.
3. Laminate the game boards to make them last longer. Make a spinner with a large headed paper fastener and a paper clip. Straighten the outside loop of the paper clip. Put the paper fastener through the loop that is left and then through the center of the spinner on the game board.
4. Students should be in groups of three or four.

Procedure
1. Distribute copies of *Balance Your Charges* and have students cut out the negative charges.
2. Distribute a game board and playing pieces to each group.
3. Students select one game piece each and color the balloon on the activity sheet the same color.
4. Explain the rules and play the game. Announce or agree upon a time period, so that the person in each group with the most nearly balanced balloon can be declared the winner.
a. Each player begins with a balanced balloon, equal numbers of positive and negative charges. Place a negative charge on top of each positive charge. Put the extra charges in the middle of the game board. Place playing pieces on GO.
b. Students spin; the player with the highest number plays first. This player spins again, moves accordingly, reads the information on the space, and follows the directions. If you gain negative charges, you draw them from the game board. If you lose negative charges, you remove them from your own balloon and add them to the "pool" on the game board. If you have extra negative charges, store them on your balloon.

Discussion
1. What makes a balloon balanced electrically?
2. What kind of static charge is on a balloon with more negative charges than positive ones?
3. What charge is on a balloon with more positive charges than negative ones?
4. What can make the balloon gain negative charges?
5. What can make the balloon lose negative charges?

Extensions
Have each group design new spaces for the game.

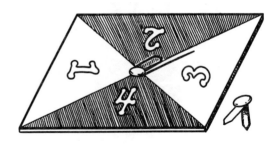

Balance Your Charges

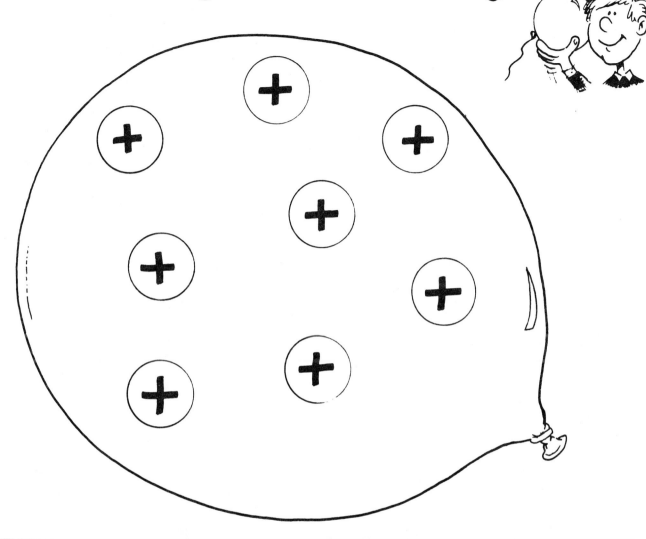

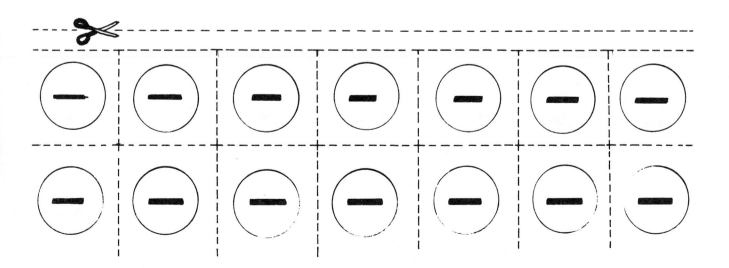

FREE CHARGES

Pick up as many electrons as you want from your pile of extra charges.

---

take one **ELECTRON**

When rubbed, WOOL takes electrons and NYLON gives electrons. You are wearing wool, the person on your left is wearing nylon.

Go BACK 4 SPACES.

Your balloon sticks to the wall. It loses **2** negative charges

---

Your balloons bump against the doorknob. **Oops!** Lose 3 negative charges

---

You get an "**A**" your electricity test take 2 negative charges from any player.

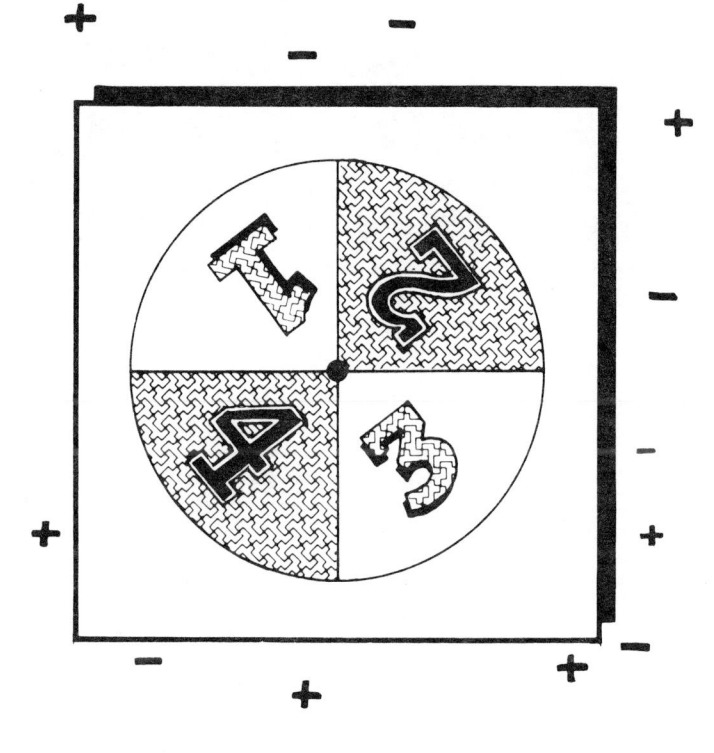

Cool windy day. Gain two negative charges

SPILLED WATER

Your balloon gets **WET** and loses **2** negative charges.

YOU RUB BALLOON **HAIR.**

GAIN 2 negative

YOUR
BALL OON
POPPED!

LOSE **2** negative charges.

WET, STORMY DAY

LOSE ELECTRONS

give up as many electrons as you want from your pile of negative charges.

BALANCE YOUR CHARGE ACCOUNT

You walk across thick carpet with your tennis shoes on

gain negative charges

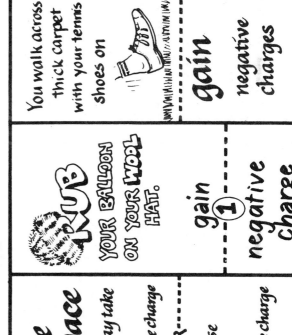

RUB YOUR BALLOON ON YOUR WOOL HAT.

gain **1** negative charge

Free Space

You may take 1 negative charge — OR — lose 1 negative charge

THE
ON YOUR

charges.

YOUR BALLOON RUBS AGAINST THE CARPET

GAIN **2** NEGATIVE CHARGES

GO

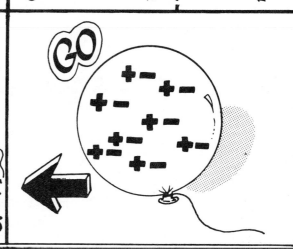

Nature's Light and Sound Show

Topic Area
Lightning - speed of light and sound

Introductory Statement
Students will determine how far away lightning is by counting the number of seconds between seeing the flash of lightning and hearing its thunder.

Math	Science
Problem solving	Observing
Computing	Collecting data
Measuring time	Generalizing
Writing formulas	Applying
Sequencing	Making and testing hypotheses

Materials
magnetic compass
clock that ticks

Key Question
When you see lightning and hear thunder, which reaches you first, the light or the sound?

Background Information
The flash of light we see when lightning strikes travels at the speed of light. The lightning itself (which is electrical) travels just a bit more slowly. The speed of light is approximately 300,000 kilometers per second or 186,000 miles per second. The speed of light varies with the medium it is traveling through and is fastest in a vacuum. Light is slowed very slightly by air.

Thunder is caused by the shock wave that occurs when lightning superheats the air around it. Since thunder is sound, it travels at the speed of sound. The speed of sound is approximately 1200 kilometers per hour or 750 miles per hour. The speed of sound in air varies with the temperature, atmospheric pressure, and several other factors.

Since the flash and thunder caused by lightning occur almost simultaneously but travel at different speeds, the distance lightning is from an observer can be found by finding the difference in time between the flash and the thunder. Since the flash of lightning travels at such great speed (fast enough to travel around the world almost eight times in one second), we can say that it reaches a viewer almost instantaneously. The much slower thunder, which travels at the speed of sound, takes longer to reach an observer. When the flash of lightning is seen, the thunder will be traveling to the observer at about 1200 kilometers (750 miles) per hour. This is about 333 meters per second or a kilometer every three seconds (1100 feet per second or about a mile every five seconds).

To find how far away lightning is in kilometers, an observer counts the number of seconds between seeing the flash of lightning and hearing its thunder, then divides this number by three. For example, if there are 13 seconds between seeing the lightning and hearing its thunder, it would be a little over four kilometers away. To find the distance in miles, the time would be divided by five. Thus a difference of 15 seconds between the lightning and the thunder would mean that the lightning is about three miles away.

Management
1. Calculators can be used with this lesson.
2. This lesson was designed to be done using metric units. It can be done using standard units by substituting the equivalent values from the information above.
3. In tracking a storm with *Page 3*, use cooperative learning groups. We suggest the following roles:
   Student #1: observes lightning, calls out a prearranged signal, and points in that direction
   Student #2: on the chart draws a straight, colored line from the center out in that direction
   Student #3: at the signal, starts counting seconds until thunder is heard
   Student #4: records the number of seconds, computes the distance, and records this on the table
   Student #2: on the chart records a black "X" on the line at the approximate distance from the center.

Procedure
1. As a class, share information and experiences related to lightning and lightning storms. When the dangers of lightning are mentioned, agree that lightning can be dangerous because it is electrical, but that just as we use electricity and use it safely, we can observe and study lightning without danger. Caution students not to stand outdoors to observe lightning; if they are caught outdoors, they should go into a building. (See *Safety Zone* fact sheet.)
2. Pass out the first two pages and discuss the *Key Question*: "When you see lightning and hear thunder, which reaches you first, the light or the sound?"
3. Work through the the first page. The speed of light is commonly given in kilometers per second and the speed of sound in kilometers per hour. To compare the two, it is necessary for students to learn how to express them in the same terms. Have students calculate the distance sound travels per minute (20 km) and per second ($1/3$ or $0.3\overline{3}$ km).
4. Work through the upper part of *Page 2*, guiding students as they start to realize the vast difference between the speeds of light and sound.
5. Storm simulation: In order to track a real lightning

Nature's Light and Sound Show

Topic Area
Lightning - speed of light and sound

Introductory Statement
Students will determine how far away lightning is by counting the number of seconds between seeing the flash of lightning and hearing its thunder.

Math	**Science**
Problem solving	Observing
Computing	Collecting data
Measuring time	Generalizing
Writing formulas	Applying
Sequencing	Making and testing hypotheses

Materials
magnetic compass
clock that ticks

Key Question
When you see lightning and hear thunder, which reaches you first, the light or the sound?

Background Information
The flash of light we see when lightning strikes travels at the speed of light. The lightning itself (which is electrical) travels just a bit more slowly. The speed of light is approximately 300,000 kilometers per second or 186,000 miles per second. The speed of light varies with the medium it is traveling through and is fastest in a vacuum. Light is slowed very slightly by air.

Thunder is caused by the shock wave that occurs when lightning superheats the air around it. Since thunder is sound, it travels at the speed of sound. The speed of sound is approximately 1200 kilometers per hour or 750 miles per hour. The speed of sound in air varies with the temperature, atmospheric pressure, and several other factors.

Since the flash and thunder caused by lightning occur almost simultaneously but travel at different speeds, the distance lightning is from an observer can be found by finding the difference in time between the flash and the thunder. Since the flash of lightning travels at such great speed (fast enough to travel around the world almost eight times in one second), we can say that it reaches a viewer almost instantaneously. The much slower thunder, which travels at the speed of sound, takes longer to reach an observer. When the flash of lightning is seen, the thunder will be traveling to the observer at about 1200 kilometers (750 miles) per hour. This is about 333 meters per second or a kilometer every three seconds (1100 feet per second or about a mile every five seconds).

To find how far away lightning is in kilometers, an observer counts the number of seconds between seeing the flash of lightning and hearing its thunder, then divides this number by three. For example, if there are 13 seconds between seeing the lightning and hearing its thunder, it would be a little over four kilometers away. To find the distance in miles, the time would be divided by five. Thus a difference of 15 seconds between the lightning and the thunder would mean that the lightning is about three miles away.

Management
1. Calculators can be used with this lesson.
2. This lesson was designed to be done using metric units. It can be done using standard units by substituting the equivalent values from the information above.
3. In tracking a storm with *Page 3*, use cooperative learning groups. We suggest the following roles:
   Student #1: observes lightning, calls out a prearranged signal, and points in that direction
   Student #2: on the chart draws a straight, colored line from the center out in that direction
   Student #3: at the signal, starts counting seconds until thunder is heard
   Student #4: records the number of seconds, computes the distance, and records this on the table
   Student #2: on the chart records a black "X" on the line at the approximate distance from the center.

Procedure
1. As a class, share information and experiences related to lightning and lightning storms. When the dangers of lightning are mentioned, agree that lightning can be dangerous because it is electrical, but that just as we use electricity and use it safely, we can observe and study lightning without danger. Caution students not to stand outdoors to observe lightning; if they are caught outdoors, they should go into a building. (See *Safety Zone* fact sheet.)
2. Pass out the first two pages and discuss the *Key Question*: "When you see lightning and hear thunder, which reaches you first, the light or the sound?"
3. Work through the the first page. The speed of light is commonly given in kilometers per second and the speed of sound in kilometers per hour. To compare the two, it is necessary for students to learn how to express them in the same terms. Have students calculate the distance sound travels per minute (20 km) and per second (1/3 or $0.3\overline{3}$ km).
4. Work through the upper part of *Page 2*, guiding students as they start to realize the vast difference between the speeds of light and sound.
5. Storm simulation: In order to track a real lightning

storm, students need to learn to count seconds with some degree of accuracy. Use a ticking clock to help them count "one one-thousand, two one-thousand..." until they can do this.

6. To simulate the lightning, flash the classroom lights. Students begin counting. Prepare some kind of noise to simulate the thunder. When the thunder sounds at three seconds, students record the three, then explain that they are dividing by three to compute the distance in kilometers. (Repeatedly help them to see that every three second gap between lightning flash and thunder represents 1 kilometer.)

7. Use *Page 3* to track a real storm. (See *Management Suggestions* for student roles.) For safety, do this from indoors. If you do not have lightning storms in your area, you may simulate a storm in the same way that one was simulated using *Page 2*. Be sure to make the line colored and the "X" black, so that the chart does not become cluttered with marks. The important part of the chart is to see how the storm has moved by observing the pattern of "X"s. (We are indebted to Dr. Verne R. Rockcastle of Cornell University for this strategy of tracking storms.)

Discussion
1. Which travels faster, light or sound?
2. How do you know?
3. Can you think of some other examples where you see something before you hear it?
4. If you hear thunder at almost the same time that you see lightning, what does that tell you?

Extensions
1. Do the activity substituting miles for kilometers.
2. Have students go to a track meet and calculate the speed of sound. This can be done if they stand a known distance from the starting gun and use a stopwatch. By watching for the puff of smoke from the gun and timing how long it takes to hear the bang, the speed of sound can be calculated.

Curriculum Correlations
Language arts: Have students read more about lightning and write a report on their findings.
Social studies: Research Benjamin Franklin and his study of lightning.

Nature's Light and Sound Show - Page 1

A lightning storm is an electrical event.
Lightning is a huge electrical spark that causes
a flash we see and thunder we hear.

When we see lightning, it is fun to know how far away it is. We can do this by finding out how long it takes for the sight and sound to reach our eyes and ears.

Since light travels very fast, its speed is difficult to measure. Instead, we will work with the sound, the thunder.

> • Sound travels about 1200 <u>kilometers per hour.</u>

How far does sound travel per <u>minute</u>?
There are 60 minutes in each hour.
Divide 1200 by 60.

> • Sound travels about _____ <u>kilometers per minute.</u>

How far does sound travel per <u>second</u>?
There are 60 seconds in each minute.
Divide your <u>kilometers per minute</u> by 60.

> • Sound travels about _____ <u>kilometers per second.</u>

If light travels about 300,000 km per second and sound travels
_____ km per second, which would reach you first?

Explain your answer. _____

_____

Nature's Light and Sound Show - Page 2

How far away is the storm? If there is lightning, we can answer this question by figuring out how far away the lightning is.

Sound travels about 1/3 (0.3$\overline{3}$) kilometer per second.
How far will sound travel in 3 seconds? _____ kilometer(s)

If you see the flash of lightning and then hear the thunder 3 seconds later, how far away is the lightning? _____ kilometer(s)

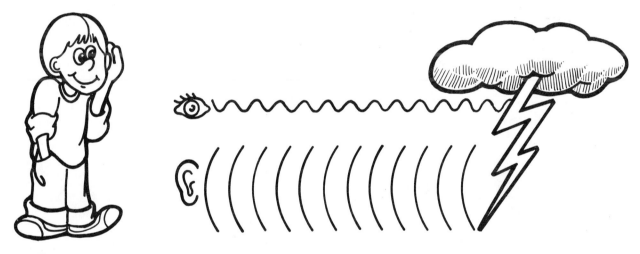

Now let's practice tracking a storm.

Count the seconds between the flash of lightning and the sound of the thunder. Use this table to record your data.

Time difference in seconds	÷ ___	Distance in km
	÷ ___	
	÷ ___	
	÷ ___	

Congratulations!
You are a storm tracker!

Nature's Light and Sound Show - Page 3

Let's track a real storm.   Here is a chart and a table to help you.

1. Place the chart so that it is correctly aligned with north. When there is a flash of lightning, note the location. Is it north of you? …southeast? …west? Draw a colored line from the center (you) out in that direction.

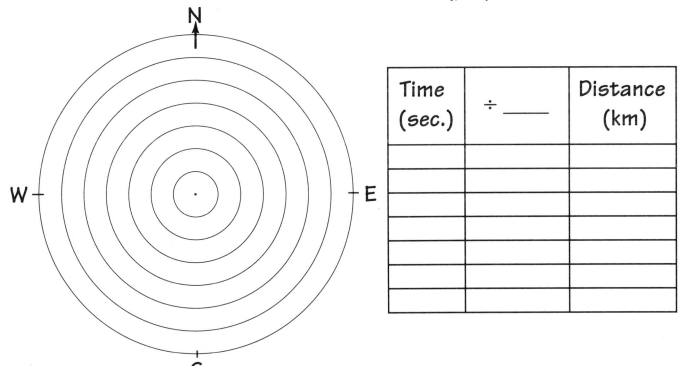

Time (sec.)	÷ _____	Distance (km)

2. Count the seconds and find out how far away the lightning is. Record data on the table.

3. On the chart, put a black X on the line to show how far away the lightning is.

4. Continue to observe lightning and record its location. Remember, the lightning may not be in the center of the storm.

What did you learn? _____

_____

_____

22   © 1991 AIMS Education Foundation

Lightning

Lightning is a very interesting phenomenon of nature. It is a huge electrical spark. We usually see it going from a cloud to the ground, but it also travels between two clouds, within a cloud, and even from a cloud into the air.

During a storm, many actions are taking place. Wind is blowing, water is freezing, and ice is melting. Raindrops are forming, dividing, and being blown by the wind. Ice crystals and raindrops collide and become positively or negatively charged. Latest research shows that the positively charged particles gather near the top and bottom of the cloud, while the negatively charged particles are sandwiched in between.

The cloud's lower negative particles induce a positive charge on the earth's surface. When the voltage in the cloud is large enough to ionize the air and make it a conductor, the built-up negative charges surge toward the earth in a series of faint, jagged streaks known as <u>leaders</u>.

Since opposite charges attract each other, these positive charges surge up to meet the leaders' negative charges. This surge continues upward, retracing the leader's paths back to the cloud in bright <u>return strokes</u> we see and call "lightning."

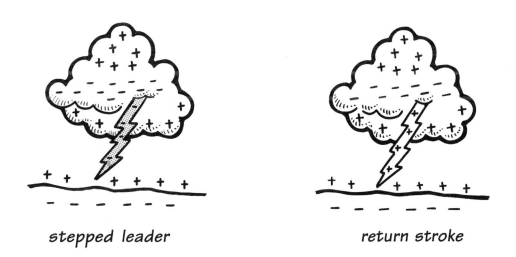

stepped leader   return stroke

Although each flash of lightning lasts only about a millionth of a second, it has a huge amount of electric current in it. Some single flashes have been measured at over 300,000 amperes of electricity, enough to light about 200,000 homes. The light from these return strokes of lightning travel at the speed of light (300,000 kilometers per second), while the electrical charges in them move just a bit more slowly.

As lightning travels through the air, it heats the air in its path to over 60,000 degrees, Fahrenheit. This superheated air expands very quickly, producing a wave of pressure that causes thunder.

Since lightning strikes somewhere on the earth about 100 times each second, there are frequent opportunities to study it. Because we know more and more about the conditions under which lightning is most apt to happen, high-speed cameras have been designed to sense these conditions and automatically photograph the lightning when it happens.

Although many scientists have investigated what it is and how it works, lightning is still very difficult to analyze and understand. This is because the information related to it ranges from the action of tiny atoms to the production of huge amounts of heat and light. This is why you may read conflicting information in different books. Since scientists are discovering more and more about lightning all the time, reading current magazines like Scientific American is a good way to get the latest accurate information.

Lightning - Sequencing Activity

Read the Lightning fact sheet (Pages 1-3), and then put these diagrams in proper sequence.

Lightning strikes.

The wind blows causing updrafts and downdrafts in the cloud.

Water droplets collide with ice crystals.

Negative charges in the cloud induce a positive charge on the ground.

The particles become charged and separate within the cloud.

Static Extensions

These activities work best in a cool, dry environment; otherwise, the static charges quickly dissipate.

☞ Give students small pieces of scratch paper 5x7 cm and have them scuff their feet on a carpet and then place the paper flat against several surfaces. Observe what happens. The paper will stick to some surfaces and not others. When it sticks to a surface, the charge on the paper induces an opposite charge in the surface to which it sticks.

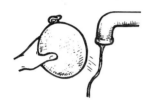

☞ Have students rub their hair (it should be clean and dry) with a balloon. Have them hold the balloon near a thin, steady stream of water from a faucet. Observe the results. The negative charge on the balloon will induce a positive charge in the stream of water. The opposite charges attract and the path of the water is bent toward the balloon.

☞ Rub nylon stockings with plastic wrap. Observe what happens. The stockings will gain a positive charge and since like charges repel the stockings will "fill up."

☞ Blow soap bubbles and attract them with a charged balloon or comb.

☞ Use static electricity to overcome gravity by sticking charged balloons on the wall or ceiling.

☞   Put a piece of paper on the wall and rub it with nylon or plastic wrap, see which makes it stick to the wall the longest.

☞   Rub various plastic straws or pens with nylon or a paper towel. Depending on the type of plastic they are made of, some will gain a strong negative charge and act as "magic wands," attracting small bits of paper, styrofoam, salt, etc.

☞   In a darkened room, pull some tape off a roll of electric tape, watch the static sparks.

☞   Hang a banana from a string. Charge a balloon and bring it near the banana. The balloon will induce an opposite charge in the near part of the banana. The banana will twist and follow the balloon.

☞   Borrow a Van de Graaff generator from a high school science teacher and let your students have a hair-raising experience!

Sparky's Light Kit

Topic Area
Electric circuits

Introductory Statement
Students will experiment with a bulb, a D cell, and a large paper clip (or wire) to make a bulb light.

Math	**Science**
Problem solving	Observing
	Drawing conclusions

Materials
For each group:
plastic bag containing
    D cell
    flashlight bulb
    jumbo paper clip or wire (10-15 cm)

Key Question
How can you make a bulb light using a bulb, a D cell, and a jumbo paper clip or wire?

Background Information
If a flashlight bulb is placed correctly in a complete circuit so that electricity passes through it, it will light. In order for current to flow through the bulb it must be connected to the circuit at two points, the *tip contact* (the metal button at the bottom of the bulb) and the *base contact* (the metal side of the bulb's base). To make the bulb light with the materials above, either the base contact or the tip contact of the bulb must touch one terminal of the D cell. The paper clip or wire must connect the cell's other terminal to the remaining contact. One way to do this is shown in the illustration below.

Management
1. Students should be in groups of two.
2. Test bulbs and cells beforehand to be sure they are working.
3. The batteries, bulbs, and paper clips should be put into bags ahead of time. Each group receives one bag.

Procedure
1. Pass out a plastic bag and activity sheets to each group.
2. Challenge the students to make the bulb light using only the materials in the bag.
3. After students have made the bulb light, challenge them to find another way to light the bulb using the same materials.
4. Have students draw pictures showing two ways they lit their bulbs.
5. Discuss the results.

Discussion
1. How many ways can we light the bulb with these materials?
2. What other materials could we use instead of the paper clip [wire]?
3. Will the bulb light with a different size cell?

Sparky's DO IT YOURSELF LIGHT KIT

Draw pictures that show <u>two</u> ways you lit the bulb...

30

Path Finders

Topic Area
Electric circuits

Introductory Statement
Students will learn about complete and incomplete circuits by trying to light a bulb using various systems of bulbs, wires, and cells (batteries).

Math
Graphing

Science
Observing
Predicting
Collecting and organizing data
Drawing conclusions

Materials
Per group:
 D cell
 flashlight bulb
 2 10-15 cm wires
 scissors
 red and yellow crayons or markers
 glue

Key Question
How can you make a complete electric circuit that will light a bulb?

Background Information

> A complete circuit is a series of wires and/or electrical devices that form a closed path through which electricity can flow.

To work, a circuit needs a source of electrical energy. The source of electricity used in this investigation is the cell, better known to most people (incorrectly) as a battery.

> A cell is a single unit containing electrodes and an electrolyte for producing electricity. A battery is made up of two or more cells joined together.

If an incandescent bulb is placed in a complete circuit so that the electricity passes through it, it will light. Incandescent bulbs have two thick wires supporting a thin, tightly coiled, conducting filament which glows when electricity flows through it. (Edison's original bulb used sewing thread for the filament!) To make the bulb a part of the circuit, one of the circuit wires must be touching the bottom tip of the bulb's base, and the other must touch the side of the bulb's base. Any system which causes the bulb to light is a complete circuit.

Management
1. Sparky's Light Kit may be used before this activity to provide some experience with circuits.
2. This activity works best if students work in groups of two or three.
3. Beforehand, make sure that all the cells and bulbs are functioning.
4. Although D cells work best for this activity, C or AA cells can also be used.
5. Insulation should be stripped off about two centimeters at the ends of the wires so that a good connection can be made. Narrow strips of aluminum foil can be substituted for the wire.

Procedure
Part 1
1. Show students a cell, two wires, and a bulb. Discuss the *Key Question:* "How can you make a complete electric circuit that will light a bulb?"
2. Give each group a cell, wires, and a bulb; challenge them to get their bulb to light. Allow time for exploration so that students may test various circuits. Help any groups that have trouble.
3. Have each successful group show and explain what they did.
4. Pass out red crayons and the activity sheets. Have students predict which of the pictured systems will light; identify these by drawing a star on them.
5. Have students build each system pictured and observe whether or not it lights the bulb. Diagrams A, E, G, and H depict complete circuits. Color yellow the diagram of each arrangement that worked.
6. When groups have finished testing all the systems, discuss the results.
Part 2
1. Distribute scissors, glue, and the activity sheet. Explain that students should cut out each of the systems on the *Part 1* sheet and glue them on this sheet, diagrams of complete circuits in the *Lights R Us* store and incomplete circuits in *Sparky's Fix It Shop*.
2. Have each group think how Sparky can make the incomplete circuits work. Groups can test these predictions and draw in the necessary changes.
Part 3
1. Pass out the third activity sheet, *REPAIR MANUAL*. Have groups discuss why the systems pictures won't work and then how they could be fixed. Record this information on the sheet.
2. As a class, share methods of fixing each of the non-working systems.

Discussion
1. What are the similarities of the systems that work?
2. What are the similarities of the systems that don't work?
3. Is electricity flowing through the systems that make the bulb light? How do you know?
4. Is electricity flowing through the systems that don't make the bulb light? How do you know?
5. What do you think are necessary elements of all complete circuits?

Extensions
1. Make as many different complete circuits as possible using the materials provided.
2. Test other materials that can be substituted for the wire.
3. Make a switch that turns the bulb on and off.
4. Use a battery (two or more cells linked together) as a part of the circuit and note the difference in the brightness of the bulb. Warn students that bulbs burn out more quickly when more cells are added.

Curriculum Correlations
Language arts: Write a story about working in *Sparky's Fix It Shop.*
Social studies: Discuss how the electric light has changed our daily life. Read about how the light bulb was invented. Read a biography of Thomas Edison. What else did he invent? Since he is thought to have had a learning disability, discuss his achievements in the light of his limitations.

Name _____

1. MAKE A PREDICTION. PUT A STAR ON THE ONES YOU THINK WILL LIGHT.

2. TEST, THEN COLOR IN THE BULBS THAT DID LIGHT UP.

PATH FINDERS

A.

B.

C.

D.

E.

F.

G.

H.

I.

FIND NEW WAYS TO LIGHT THE BULBS. DRAW THEM HERE. YOU MAY WORK WITH A PARTNER.

Name _____

Part 2

PATH FINDERS

SPARKY'S FIX IT SHOP

Lights R Us

REPAIR MANUAL

Tell why these circuits will not work...

Circuit Quiz Boards

Topic Area
Electric circuits

Introductory Statement
Students will construct a circuit quiz board.

Math
Sequencing

Science
Observing
Collecting and organizing data
Recording data

Materials
Per student or group:
file folder (old ones are OK)
C or D cell
miniature Christmas light
10 strips of aluminum foil 1 cm x 30 cm
roll of masking tape
2 30-35 cm pieces of wire with ends stripped
hole punch
scissors
rubber band

Key Question
How can we build a quiz board that will light up when a question is linked with the correct answer?

Background Information
The quiz board works like an old-fashioned phone switchboard. Each question is connected to the correct answer by a strip of aluminum foil. The aluminum foil is covered by masking tape to insulate it and prevent short circuits. When a correct question and answer are chosen, it completes the circuit, causing the bulb to light.

Management
1. Have a sample of the quiz board made up beforehand to show students how it is constructed.
2. The miniature Christmas lights work best for this activity. If you use a flashlight bulb and holder you will need an extra short piece of wire to go from the battery to the bulb holder.
3. Oak tag or pieces of poster board can be substituted for the file folders. The advantage of the file folders is that the electric connections are hidden when the folder is closed.
4. You may have students work individually or in groups to research the questions and construct the quiz boards.
5. Students can make more than one question-and-answer sheet and use the board more than once.
6. The topics for the quiz board questions and answers (such as math facts, science content, history facts, etc.) can given to the students or chosen by them.

Procedure
1. Show students a sample quiz board and demonstrate how it works. Tell students that they will be building similar boards. Discuss how the quiz boards work.
2. Have students write out 10 questions with answers.
3. Distribute copies of the blank question and answer sheet. Have students copy their questions in the left column; then have them change the order of the answers and copy them in the right column.
4. Using file folders, have students glue or tape the question-and-answer sheet securely to the folder front. Use a hole punch to make a hole next to each question and answer. The holes on the right side of the folder should only go through the front cover and the template, not the back cover.
5. Inside the folder, draw lines from the hole for each question to the hole for the matching answer. These will be guidelines for the foil strips.
6. Distribute aluminum foil strips, scissors, and masking tape. Place a foil strip over each guideline so that the foil extends beyond the hole, trimming as necessary; tape foil strip ends to cover the holes; then place tape on top of the foil strip (make sure no foil is showing). Repeat this process until all foil strips have been placed and taped. When taping is finished, no foil should be visible except from the front through the holes.

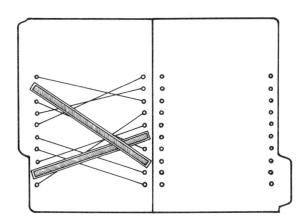

7. Distribute the cells, bulbs, and wires. Tape a long wire to the negative (flat) end of the cell. Then tape the wire end from the light to the positive end. To help ensure good contact, wind a rubber band lengthwise around the cell. Carefully tape the cell onto the question and answer sheet. Attach the second long wire to the other wire from the bulb. Anchor the bulb by taping wires on both sides of it.

8. Have students test their quiz boards by touching the wire from the bulb to the foil (showing through the hole) beside the first question, while simultaneously touching the wire from the battery to the foil beside the corresponding answer. The bulb should light.

9. After students have tested their boards, they can exchange them with other students.

Discussion

1. Why does the bulb light when the right question and answer are touched by the two wires?
2. How can you use the same board for other sets of questions and answers?
3. Why is the masking tape so important?
4. How is this quiz board like the wiring in a house?

Extensions

1. Design a circuit quiz board that uses a buzzer instead of a light.
2. Design a way to change the questions and answers on the quiz board easily.
3. Design a way to change the positions of the question-answer combinations on the quiz board.

Curriculum Correlations

All curriculum areas: Make question and answer sheets to go with other areas of the curriculum.

Circuit Quiz Board

Name_____

1.			A.
2.			B.
3.			C.
4.			D.
5.			E.
6.			F.
7.			G.
8.			H.
9.			I.
10.			J.

ELECTRICAL CONNECTIONS   37   © 1991 AIMS Education Foundation

Wet Cell Battery

Caution: This is for demonstration only. It should be set up by the teacher under a hood or in a well-ventilated area.

Topic Area
Chemical and electrical energy

Introductory Statement
This is a demonstration in which students observe how chemical energy is converted into electrical energy in a wet cell battery.

Science
Observing
Predicting
Drawing conclusions

Materials
quart bottle of bleach
one pound box of baking soda
paper towels
aluminum foil
2 quart jars or beakers
plastic wrap
flashlight bulb and bulb holder
3 - 80 cm pieces of 20 gauge *uninsulated* copper wire

Key Question
How does chemical energy change into electrical energy?

Background Information
A battery is a device that produces electrical potential energy through chemical action. Batteries are made up of two or more electric cells joined together. Each cell contains everything necessary to produce electricity. Two common types of cells are the wet cell and the dry cell. As the name implies, wet cells contain chemicals in a liquid form. Dry cells are not really dry, but contain chemicals in a pastelike form.

Each cell in a battery has two electrodes made of different types of chemically active materials (common dry cells use zinc and carbon for the electrodes). Each cell also contains an electrolyte (in the form of a liquid or paste) which connects the two electrodes and acts as a conductor of the current inside the cell. The type of chemical reaction in a cell depends on the type of cell, but all produce ions and electrons. In a carbon-zinc dry cell, zinc atoms oxidize and give up electrons, thus becoming positive ions. In doing this they move away from the zinc electrode, leaving the electrons behind. This causes a net negative charge to form at that electrode. If the cell is connected to an electric circuit, then the electrons flow through the circuit producing an electric current.

In this activity, the aluminum foil and copper wire form the two electrodes and the bleach acts as the electrolyte. The aluminum oxidizes and positive aluminum ions go into solution in the bleach, leaving an excess of electrons on the aluminum electrode. When the two cells are connected to the light bulb, the electrons are able to flow and produce an electric current.

Management
1. The demonstration should be set up where it can be observed easily.
2. Cover the top of each jar with plastic wrap to reduce the smell of the bleach.
3. A miniature Christmas light may be used in place of the bulb and holder.

Procedure
1. Cut two pieces of foil 10cm by 30cm. Roll up each piece, crumple one end, and place it in the jar (see illustration).
2. Put a double thick 10-12 cm square piece of paper towel on top of the crumpled end of each piece of foil to act as an insulator.
3. Attach the three copper wires in the following manner:
   Wire #1: Wind one end of the wire around the top of the aluminum foil in Jar A. Attach the other end to the bulb holder.
   Wire #2: Attach one end of the wire to the bulb holder. Curl the rest of the wire into a ball and place it on top of the paper towel in Jar B.
   Wire #3: Wind one end of the wire around the top of the aluminum foil in Jar B. Curl the rest of the wire into a ball and place it on top of the paper towel in Jar A. *Make sure the wire and aluminum foil do not touch or they will cause a short circuit.*
4. Pour bleach (which acts as an electrolyte) into each jar until it comes up and completely covers the ball of wire. The paper towel will get wet and allow the bleach to pass through, while keeping the aluminum and copper from touching. The bulb should begin to glow and continue glowing for several hours until the chemical reaction stops.
5. Add a teaspoon of baking soda to the bleach at the top of each jar; the bulb will glow more brightly for a short time. [The baking soda temporarily increases the conductivity of the electrolyte (bleach), allowing more current to flow through the circuit.]

Discussion
1. How does a wet cell battery work?
2. How can we keep the battery going for a longer time period? [add more bleach]
3. Why is a wet cell dangerous to handle? [it contains chemicals that are potentially dangerous]
4. What will cause the battery to stop producing electricity? [the chemical reaction stops]

Extensions
1. Use a volt meter to find the voltage of the battery.
2. Cut apart a carbon-zinc dry cell (don't use an alkaline cell for this) and examine the parts.

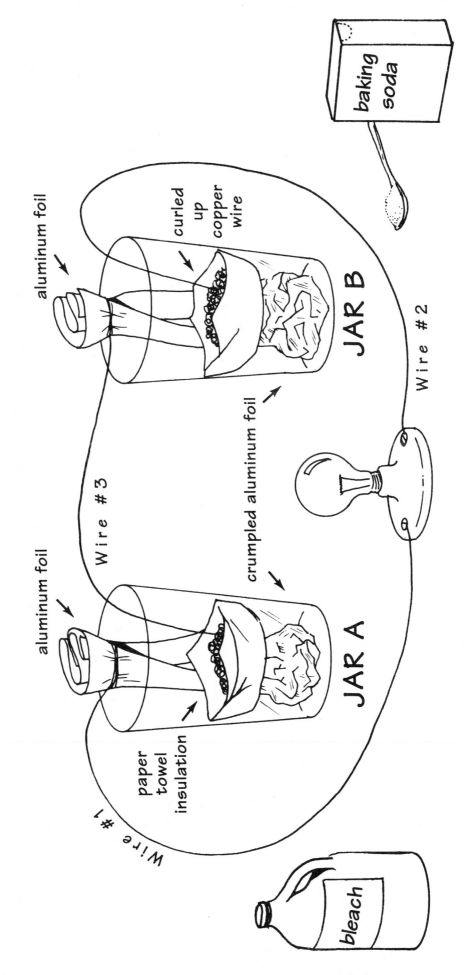

Wet Cell Battery

Conductor or Insulator?

Topic Area
Electric conductors and insulators

Introductory Statement
Students will test a variety of materials to determine if they are conductors or insulators.

Math
Venn diagrams

Science
Predicting
Observing
Drawing conclusions

Materials
Per group:
1   15-25 cm wire with ends stripped
D cell
flashlight bulb
tape
materials to be tested (see activity sheet)

Key Question
What materials will conduct electricity?

Background Information
A direct electric current is a steady flow of electric charges through a medium called a *conductor*. In solid conductors (which include all metals), it is the negatively charged electrons that flow and make up the electric current. Metals have some electrons that are not tightly bound to any single atom; they are free to move about from atom to atom. These electrons are called *conducting electrons*.

Positive charges do not flow in a solid conductor, since the positively charged protons are bound within the nuclei of atoms. These atoms are locked in the grid-like structure of the solid material and are not free to move. Therefore, the current in a solid conductor is caused by the movement of negative electric charges (electrons).

In liquids that conduct electricity, the electric charges that flow can be positive, negative, or both. The negative charges are provided by either free electrons or *negative ions* (atoms or molecules with extra electrons). The positive charges are provided by *positive ions* (atoms or molecules that are missing electrons).

Materials that do not normally conduct electricity are called *insulators*. Other materials that conduct electricity to a lesser degree than conductors, but more than insulators, are called *semiconductors*; these are of great importance in electronics. *It is important to note that at certain voltages and temperatures, all materials will conduct electricity to some degree.* Even air, which is normally an excellent insulator, will conduct electric charges when the voltage is high enough; lightning illustrates this. The only perfect insulator is a vacuum.

Management
1. Students should work in groups of two to four.
2. Beforehand, make a sample circuit to test the conductivity of materials and show students.

Procedure
Part 1
1. Distribute materials to each group.
2. Show students how to build a circuit to test the conductivity of materials using the D cell, wire, and light bulb.
3. For the first five objects listed, predict whether or not the object will conduct electricity. Place the object in the circuit and record the results.
4. Have students pick five additional objects to test, and repeat the above process.
5. Discuss the results and write conclusions in the space provided. Make sure that students note that some objects, like the pencil, are both conductors and insulators, depending on what part of the object is placed in the test circuit.

Part 2
1. Using *Page 1,* list the conductors and insulators in the appropriate boxes on *Page 2.*
2. Discuss common characteristics of the conductors. Record these characteristics in the space provided.
3. Discuss common characteristics of the insulators. Record these characteristics in the space provided.
4. Distribute *Page 3*. In the appropriate areas of the Venn diagram, write the names of the objects tested. Discuss the results.

Discussion
1. How are all the conductors alike?
2. How are all the insulators alike?
3. What distinguishes a conductor from an insulator?
4. Are there any objects that are both conductors and insulators? [pencil]
5. What other things do you think might be conductors?
6. What other things might be insulators?
7. Why are many wires coated with plastic or some other material?

Extensions
1. Test other objects to see if they are insulators or conductors.
2. Build a different circuit to test the conductivity of materials.
3. Build a circuit to test the conductivity of various liquids.

Curriculum Correlations
Health: Discuss the importance of insulators to health and safety. Identify some of the places insulators are used in the classroom.

Conductor or Insulator?

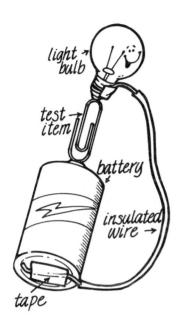

light bulb →

test item →

battery

insulated wire →

tape

A *conductor* is any item that allows electrons to flow freely through it. The light bulb should light.

An *insulator* is any item that **does not allow electrons to flow easily through it. The bulb will not light.**

Tape the wire to the bottom of the cell. Wrap the wire around the metal side of the light bulb. Tape it securely in place.

Test each item. Record your findings in the table below.

Item	Prediction	Conductor	Insulator
paper clip			
tape			
pencil			
string			
ruler			

41

Conductor or Insulator?

Conductors	Insulators
_____	_____
_____	_____
_____	_____
_____	_____
_____	_____
_____	_____
_____	_____

How are the conductors alike? _____

_____

How are the insulators alike? _____

_____

Conclusions: _____

_____

_____

Conductor or Insulator?

insulators

conductors

Make a Dimmer Switch

Topic Area
Electrical conductivity - semiconductors

Introductory Statement
Students will make a dimmer switch using a pencil lead.

Math
Measuring
Graphing

Science
Observing
Drawing conclusions

Materials
Per group:
- 2 D cells
- miniature Christmas light
- 15 cm wire with ends stripped
- tape
- metric ruler
- #2 pencil (see *Management*)
- scissors
- stapler

Key Question
How does a dimmer switch work?

Background Information
Materials are usually classified as to how well they conduct electricity. Those materials that readily conduct electricity are called *conductors*, while those that do not conduct electricity are called *insulators*. Between these two types of materials is a class of materials called *semiconductors*. Semiconductors conduct electricity, but not as well as conductors. Semiconductors are crucial to the electronics industry and are also used in household rheostats (dimmer switches). The ability of semiconductors to conduct electricity depends upon factors such as their length, thickness, and temperature. More current will travel through a short length of semiconducting material than through a long length. A dimmer switch simply changes the length of the path that the current takes through the semiconductor. As the length of the the semiconductor changes, the brightness of the bulb changes. In this activity, the graphite in pencil lead is used as a semiconductor (although pencil leads are now made of graphite mixed with clay, they are still referred to as "leads.")

Management
1. Use #2 pencils or mechanical pencil lead of the same thickness (0.5 and 0.7 mm mechanical pencil leads are too small and fragile to work well). Both are available at office or art supply stores. Be sure leads are at least 10 cm long.
2. Prepare pencils beforehand. Using a utility knife, split pencils as shown on the activity sheet, removing about half of the wood so the lead can be touched easily. If desired, tape pencils or leads to flat surfaces before using to avoid breakage; be sure test scale starts and ends within the untaped portion.
3. Beforehand, make a sample brightness indicator using a copy of the third activity sheet. Cut out pieces and assemble in numerical order, with the shortest on top. Staple together as shown.

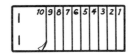

4. The brightness testing works best with the classroom lights off.
5. Work in cooperative learning groups, with these roles:
   Student #1 holds battery connections firmly.
   Student #2 moves the wire ends on the pencil lead.
   Student #3 holds the brightness indicator over the bulb and makes the readings.
   Student #4 records all data.

Procedure
1. Discuss the *Key Question:* "How does a dimmer switch work?" Explain that this activity will help them understand how dimmer switches work.
3. Distribute materials to each group and have students build the test circuit pictured on the first activity sheet.
4. Have each group make a brightness indicator (see *Management*).
5. Have students test the brightness of the bulb as the current goes through each length of pencil lead indicated and record results.
6. Discuss the results and have students write their conclusions in the space provided.
7. Have students construct a broken-line graph of their findings using the second activity sheet.

Discussion
1. Was there a difference in the brightness of the bulb as the wire was moved along the lead?
2. What might explain this difference? [different lengths of pencil lead for current to travel through]
3. In what ways is a real dimmer switch like the dimmer switch in this activity? [the length of semiconducting material that the current travels through varies as the switch is turned]

Extensions
1. Take apart an old dimmer switch and examine the parts.
2. Use different thicknesses of pencil lead and see if there is a difference.

MAKE a DIMMER Switch

How does the distance current travels through a pencil lead affect the brightness of a bulb? Make the circuit and brightness tester shown below and find out!

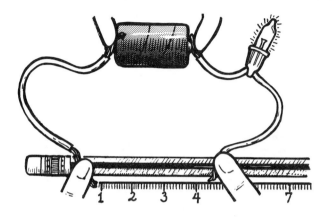

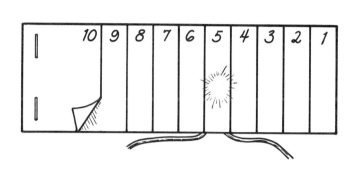

Distance Current Travels Through Pencil Lead	Brightness of Bulb as Measured by Number of Sheets of Paper Bulb Shines Through									
	1	2	3	4	5	6	7	8	9	10
10 cm										
8 cm										
6 cm										
4 cm										
2 cm										

Conclusions: _____

_____

MAKE a DIMMER Switch

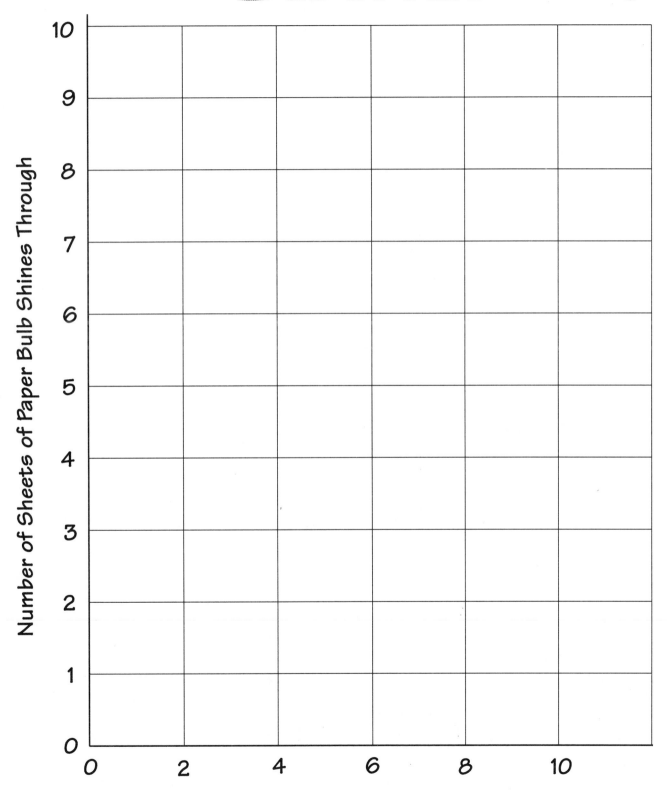

Number of Sheets of Paper Bulb Shines Through

Centimeters of Pencil Lead Current Travels Through

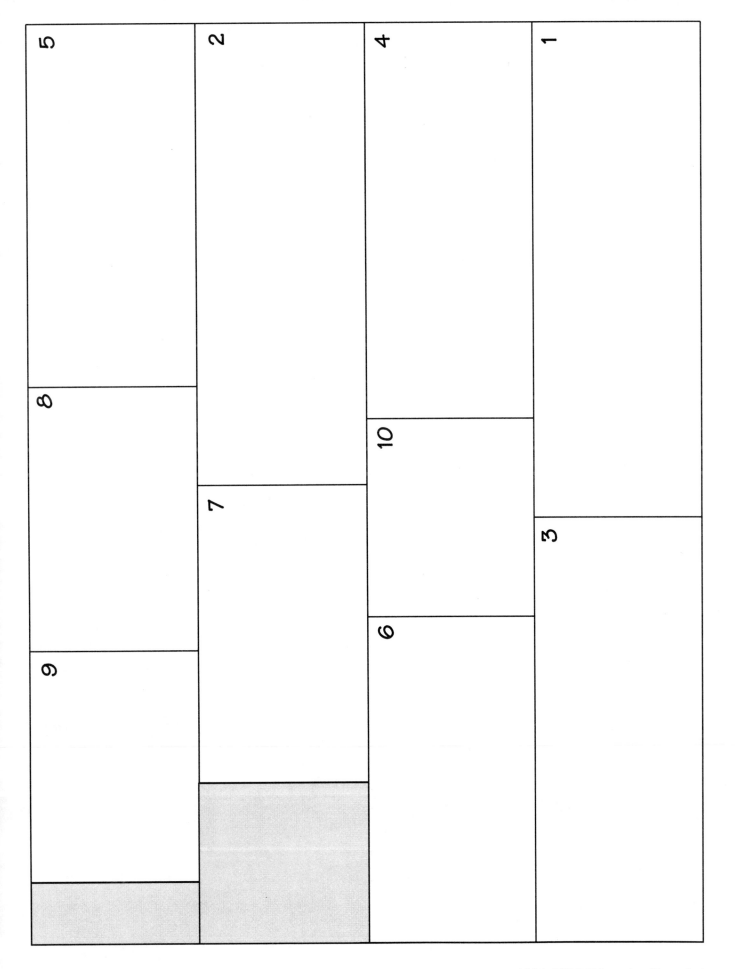

Make a Switch

Topic Area
Electric switches and circuits

Introductory Statement
Students will build simple switches to control the flow of electricity in a circuit.

Science
Observing
Drawing conclusions

Materials
For each group:
Part 1
  D cell
  3 - 15 cm wires, with ends stripped
  2 brass paper fasteners
  1.5 v bulb and holder or miniature Christmas light
  paper clip
  masking tape
  8 x 8 cm piece of tagboard
Part 2
  Above materials plus:
  2 - 10 cm wires with ends stripped
  4 more brass paper fasteners
  1 more paper clip
  1 more 8 x 8 cm piece of tagboard

Key Questions
Part 1 How can you turn the current on and off in an electrical circuit?
Part 2 How can you turn a light on from two different parts of a room?

Background Information
Most electrical devices have switches of one type or another, allowing the device to be turned on and off. An electric current will flow only if it has a complete path through which to travel. Switches are simple devices that complete or interrupt that path. When a switch is turned on (closed), it bridges a gap in the wiring, completing a path for electricity. When a switch is turned off (opened), it creates a gap in the circuit and stops the flow of electricity. Most electrical devices are controlled by a single pole switch which works like the one built in *Part 1*.

Some lights or other electrical devices are controlled by two or more switches. Those built in *Part 2* are double pole switches; they allow the device to be turned on or off from either switch.

Management
1. Students should work in groups of two or three.
2. *Part 1* and *Part 2* can be done on the same day or on separate days.
3. Make sure the brass fasteners do not touch underneath the switches. If they do, they will create a short circuit and the switches cannot be turned off.

Procedure
Part 1
1. Discuss the *Key Question*: "How can you turn the current on and off in an electrical circuit?"
2. Distribute the materials and have each group build the circuit and switch pictured. Point out similar switches in the classroom.
3. Discuss the results, and have students fill in their observations and explanations.
Part 2
1. Discuss the second *Key Question*: "How can you turn a light on from two different parts of a room?" Discuss double pole switches located either in the classroom or in students' homes. If your students live in apartments where double pole switches are not common, find some at school they can observe.
2. Build the switches and circuit as shown.
3. Follow directions to operate the switches.
4. Students may need guidance to write the explanation for how the double pole switches work.

Discussion
1. Why is it important to wrap the wire around the brass fasteners?
2. What position does the paper clip have to be in for the bulb to light?
3. Do you think all switches work the same way?
4. What is the advantage of having two double pole switches hooked up to a light?
5. What are some ways that switches are used in the classroom?
6. Why are switches important?
7. How do your switches work?

Extensions
1. Make a switch using other materials.
2. Make diagrams of all the possible switch positions (and whether or not they light the bulb) for the double pole switch circuit.
3. Using a box, make a model of a room with two doors. Wire the light using the circuit made for *Part 2* so that it can be turned on or off from either door.

Curriculum Correlations
Language arts: Remember that when students explain scientific or mathematical procedures to others, they are developing valuable skills in oral language.

Home Links
1. Have students count the number of wall and appliance switches they have at home. How many are single pole? How many are double pole?
2. Challenge students to explain double pole switches to members of their families. Share reactions to the explanations!

Part 1

How can you make an electric switch?

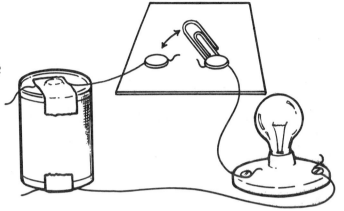

You will need these things:
- 8 x 8 cm tagboard
- 3 - 15 cm pieces of electric wire
- 2 brass paper fasteners
- 1 D cell
- 1.5 volt bulb and holder
- paper clip
- masking tape

1. Put a brass fastener through one end of the paper clip and then through the tagboard. Put the other brass fastener through the tagboard so the paper clip can touch it. Tape the ends of the brass fasteners under the tagboard so they do not touch each other.

2. Connect the wires as shown, winding them around the brass fasteners once or twice.

3. Close the switch by pressing the paper clip on the brass fastener.

What happens? _____

_____

Explain how your switch works. _____

_____

_____

_____

_____

49

Make a Switch

Part 2

How can you turn a light on from two different parts of a room?

To build double pole switches, you will need
   2 - 8 x 8 cm pieces of tagboard
   5 pieces of electric wire
     (3 - 15 cm, 2 - 10 cm)
   6 brass paper fasteners
   1 D cell
   1.5 volt bulb and holder
   2 paper clips
   masking tape
   2 crayons, different colors

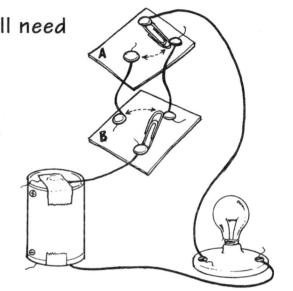

1. Set up the circuit as shown here. Tape the ends of the brass fasteners under the tagboard so they do not touch each other.

2. Try the switch in both positions until you make the bulb light. Using a crayon on this sheet, trace the path of the electric current.

3. Turn the light out at Switch A. Turn it on at Switch B. With a differently colored crayon, trace this circuit.

Explain how your double pole switches work.

_____

_____

_____

_____

_____

Circuit Breakers

Topic Area
Circuit breakers

Introductory Statement
Students will build a *circuit breaker* and learn its function as part of a circuit.

Science
Observing
Drawing conclusions

Materials
Per group:
2-3 balloons
1 paper clip switch
2-3 D cells
3 aluminum foil strips: 2-1x50 cm, 1-1x10cm
3-4 strands of steel wool, 3-5 cm
tape

Key Question
How does a circuit breaker prevent a circuit from overheating?

Background Information
A switch is one device that can complete or interrupt a circuit. Circuit breakers and fuses are other devices that do the same thing; they act as a *weak link* in a circuit because they are designed to stop the flow of electricity if the circuit becomes overloaded and begins to get too hot. These devices are crucial in helping prevent electrical fires.

Electricity flowing through a circuit will always generate some heat. The amount of heat depends on the resistance of the circuit and the amount of current present. Electrical circuits are designed to carry certain amounts of electricity without getting dangerously hot. When the amount of current in a circuit exceeds this level, fires can result. To prevent this from happening, circuit breakers and/or fuses are placed in electrical circuits; they are designed to interrupt the circuit when current exceeds safe levels.

Circuit breakers work in several different ways. The most common type uses an electromagnetic mechanism to interrupt the circuit when too much current is present. Another type uses a heat sensitive device similar to a thermostat to trigger the circuit interruption.

The *circuit breaker* built in this lesson does not work like normal circuit breakers, but it does model how a circuit breaker *breaks* a circuit and stops the current from flowing. The strands of steel wool taped to the balloon provide a greater resistance to the flow of electricity than the aluminum foil strips. This resistance heats the steel wool and melts the rubber of the balloon, causing it to pop and break the circuit. To reset the circuit breaker, the steel wool is taped to a new balloon. To change the amount of current carried by the circuit breaker before the balloon pops, the thickness and/or number of strands of steel wool can be varied. With thicker strands or more strands of steel wool, the resistance is less and the balloon will not pop as quickly.

Management
1. Students should work in groups of three or four.
2. Students can use the switch built as part of the *Make a Switch* activity.
3. The balloons should be underinflated.
4. You should try this activity before doing it with students. *Ideally, the balloon will not pop with one cell in the circuit, but will pop with two or three.*
4. If the balloon pops with only one cell, use more strands of steel wool.
5. If the balloon won't pop with three cells, try fewer strands of steel wool.

Procedure
1. Discuss the *Key Question:* "How does a circuit breaker keep a circuit from overheating?" [it interrupts the circuit when too much current is present]
2. Pass out the activity sheets and explain the procedure for making the circuit breakers.
3. Have students make the circuit shown *using only one cell. They should not have the switch closed when taping the steel wool to the balloon.*
4. Have students close the switch and observe what happens. Hopefully, most of the balloons will not pop.
5. Have students add another cell to the circuit and try again. If the balloons still don't pop, add a third cell.
6. If the balloons don't pop with three cells, check to make sure that there are no loose connections in the circuit and try again. Students may have to use fewer strands of steel wool.
7. Challenge students to make their balloons pop with more or fewer cells in the circuit.
8. Discuss the results and have students write their conclusions in the space provided.

Discussion
1. Why does the balloon pop? [the steel wool gets hot and melts the balloon]
2. How can you change your circuit breaker so that the balloon won't pop until you add more than three batteries? [increase the number of strands of steel wool - this provides more paths for the current and less resistance and heat]
3. How could you change your circuit breaker so that it would pop with only 1 battery. [use fewer strands of steel wool - this provides more resistance and heat]

Extensions
1. Hook your balloon circuit breaker to a circuit containing three lights in series. Does it pop with the same number of batteries?
2. Hook your balloon circuit breaker to a circuit containing three lights in parallel. What difference does this make?

*We would like to give special thanks to **Ron Marson** from **Tops Learning Systems** for permission to adapt this lesson from the Tops activity, **Big Bang**.*

Circuit BREAKERS

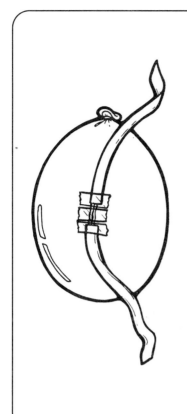

2. Tape 2 aluminum foil strips to the ends of the steel wool as shown above.

1. Blow up your balloon and tape 3 strands of steel wool to it as shown above.

4. Did the balloon pop? If not, add another cell and try again.

Challenge: Build a circuit breaker where the balloon will not pop until 3 cells are added to the circuit.

Conclusions: _____
_____
_____
_____

3. Build the circuit pictured below. Make sure the switch is open!

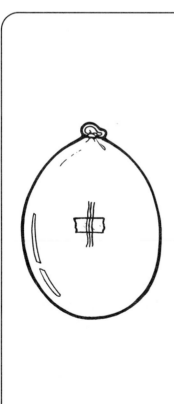

(when the circuit is done) Close the switch for 5 seconds. Then open it.

Electric Circuits

Topic Area
Series and parallel circuits

Introductory Statement
Students will build and observe series and parallel circuits.

Science
Observing
Predicting
Drawing conclusions

Materials
Per group:
2 D cells
3 flashlight bulbs and holders
7 pieces of wire, 15-20 cm
2 pieces of wire, 30-40 cm

Key Question
How does the flow of electricity in a series circuit differ from the flow in a parallel circuit?

Background Information
There are two basic types of electric circuits, *series* and *parallel*. In a series circuit, there is only one path for the current and a break in the circuit stops the current.

In a parallel circuit, there are multiple pathways or branches. If there is a break in any branch, the current will still go through the other branches. Only if all the branches have breaks will the current stop.

An added factor in any electric circuit is the resistance involved. Electrical resistance is anything that hinders the the flow of electricity. The amount of resistance in a conductor depends on the conductivity of the material, its length, thickness, and temperature. Electrical devices such as motors, transistors, and lights add resistance to a circuit. An electric bulb, for example, has much more resistance than the wires in a circuit since its filament is long, thin, and made of a material with high resistance. In circuits, the amount of current varies with the resistance. Circuits with less resistance allow more electricity to flow, while circuits with more resistance restrict the amount of current.

If three bulbs are connected in series, the current goes through each bulb in turn, and the resistance of each bulb is added to the total resistance of the circuit. Less current goes through the circuit and the bulbs glow less brightly than a single bulb would. If a bulb is removed, the path is broken and the current stops.

If three bulbs are connected in parallel, the current has multiple paths and the resistance in the circuit is reduced. Since there is less resistance, more electricity flows and each bulb glows as brightly as a single bulb. If a bulb is removed, the others stay lit since the current goes through the other branches of the circuit.

Management
1. Students should work in groups of three or four.
2. Miniature Christmas tree lights (cut apart) can be substituted for the flashlight bulbs and bulb holders.
3. Aluminum foil strips can be substituted for wires.

Procedure
Part 1
1. Distribute the materials to each group.
2. Have each group build the series circuit pictured and predict what will happen when one of the bulbs is removed. Have students remove a bulb and record the results.
3. Have students build the parallel circuit pictured and predict what will happen when a bulb is removed. Have them test their predictions and record results.
4. Have some groups replace the bulb in the parallel circuit while others rebuild the series circuit.
5. Compare the brightness of the bulbs in the two circuits. Record observations on the activity sheet.
6. Discuss the results and record conclusions.
Part 2
1. Discuss the schematic diagram and have students build the circuit pictured.
2. Have students build circuits of their own and then make schematic diagrams.
3. Students exchange diagrams and build the circuits pictured.

Discussion
1. Why did the other bulbs in the series circuit go out when one bulb was removed? [In a series circuit there is only one path for the current, and removing the bulb breaks that path and stops the current.]
2. Why did the other bulbs in the parallel circuit stay lit when one bulb was removed? [In a parallel circuit there are multiple pathways for the current, and breaking one path doesn't keep current from going through the other paths.]
3. Why are the bulbs in the parallel circuit brighter than the bulbs in the series circuit? [There are more paths for the current and less resistance in the parallel circuit.]
4. What problems might you have when lights (such as Christmas tree lights) are wired in series? [When one bulb burns out, it breaks the circuit and all the lights go off. It is often difficult to find the defective bulb, and each bulb in the series must be tested individually.]
5. What kind of circuits are most common in our homes? [parallel] Why?

Extensions
1. Try more than three bulbs in the circuits.
2. Add switches to your circuits.
3. Try different numbers of cells in the circuits.
4. Use two identical (new) cells and put one in each circuit. Leave the circuits on until both cells are dead. Compare the difference in how long they lasted.

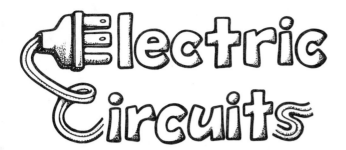

How does the flow of electricity in a series circuit differ from the flow of electricity in a parallel circuit?

1. Build a series circuit like this.

2. What happens when you remove a bulb?

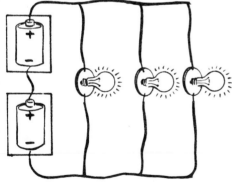

Prediction _____

_____

_____

Results _____

_____

_____

3. Build a parallel circuit like this.

4. What happens when you remove a bulb?

Prediction _____

_____

_____

Results _____

_____

_____

5. In which kind of circuit did the bulbs glow more brightly?

_____

Conclusions: _____

_____

_____

Electric Circuits - Part 2

Here is a schematic diagram of an electric circuit. Electricians use diagrams like this when they put electric circuits into houses and other buildings.

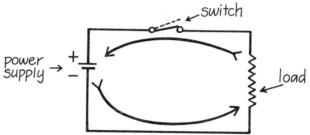

1. Build a circuit using this diagram as a plan. Use a dry cell (battery) for your power supply and a bulb for your load.

   Notice that there is a switch. When the switch is open, the circuit is broken. If you do not have a switch for your circuit, what else can you do to break the circuit and turn off your light?

   _____

   _____

2. Now make another circuit. After you have built it, make a diagram of it like the one above. See if a friend can follow your diagram and build your circuit.

55

Short Cuts

Topic Area
Electric circuits

Introductory Statement
Students will build several different parallel circuits, each with a switch, and will discover the effect on each circuit when the switch is opened and closed.

Science
Predicting
Observing
Drawing conclusions

Materials
Per group:
2 D cells
2 bulbs and holders or 2 miniature Christmas lights
1 switch
10 15-25 cm pieces of wire

Key Question
How will adding a switch to one of the branches of a parallel circuit affect the flow of electricity?

Background Information
Whenever a current flows through a circuit, it meets with resistance. The amount of resistance in a circuit is determined by one or more of these factors: the material of the wires, their length and thickness, their temperature, the type and number of electrical devices involved (bulbs, resistors, capacitors, etc.), and the type of circuit (series or parallel). In a *series circuit*, every device placed in the circuit adds resistance to the small amount present in the circuit's wires. In a *parallel circuit*, more current will flow through the branch(es) with less resistance and less current will go through the branch(es) with greater resistance.

In the parallel circuit built in *Part 1*, the switch placed in one branch changes the way that current flows; when the switch is on (closed), it provides a path with less resistance than the other two branches containing bulbs (which have a high resistance). Most of the current goes through the low resistance branch and very little goes through the two branches with the high resistance bulbs (not enough current to cause them to light). When the switch is turned off, current can no longer go through that branch; it goes through the branches with lights, and the bulbs glow. By the switch's position, the lights are turned off by turning the switch on and turned on by turning the switch off. In the first circuit in *Part 2*, the same thing happens. Even though the switch is in a different branch in this circuit, it still provides the path of least resistance when closed. It is important to note that current is flowing through both of these circuits when the switches are closed, even though the bulbs are not glowing.

In the second circuit in *Part 2*, the switch is in the same branch as one of the bulbs. In this circuit, the switch will turn the bulb in its branch on and off, while the bulb in the other branch will always be on.

In the third circuit in *Part 2*, the switch is placed between the battery and the branches of the circuit. In this circuit, the bulbs glow when the switch is closed and stop glowing when it is opened. The switch is wired in series. It is not presenting an alternate path for the current; it simply allows current to go through the circuit when it is closed and prevents current from flowing when it is open.

Electricians call an unwanted flow of electricity in a circuit a *short*. A short could also be called an *easy*, since each is an unintended path of least resistance (which sometimes is a longer path) taken by the current. The closed switches in the circuit in *Part 1* and the first one in *Part 2* are *shorts*, since they provide an easy path for the current and divert most of it from the higher resistance bulbs.

Management
Students should work in groups of three or four.

Procedure
Part 1
1. Discuss the *Key Question*: "How will adding a switch to a circuit affect the flow of electricity?"
2. Have students look at the circuit diagram and then read the four possible outcomes. Let each group guess which one of the outcomes is correct.
3. Have each group build the circuit and test it with the switch in both the open and closed positions. After finding the results, disconnect the cells so that they don't drain (when the switch is closed and the lights are off, the cells are being quickly drained by the short circuit).
4. Discuss the results, and have students write their conclusions in the space provided.
Part 2
1. Discuss the question: "How does the location of the switch affect the flow of electricity?"
2. Have students look at each circuit and predict whether the bulbs will light when the switch is on (closed). Students write their predictions and reasoning.
4. Each group builds and tests the three circuits pictured, recording the results.
5. Discuss the results as a class, and have students write conclusions.

Discussion
1. Why didn't the bulbs in the first two circuits light when the switch was closed? [The switch has less resistance than the bulbs and provides an easier path for the current, diverting most of it from the bulbs.]
2. Why did the bulbs in the first two circuits light when the switch was open? [The *easy* path was broken, forcing the electricity to go through the bulbs.]
3. What is a *short*? [a path that creates an unwanted flow of electricity in a circuit]

Extensions
1. Build other circuits with more than one switch.
2. Build a parallel circuit with bulbs of different voltage.

ELECTRICAL CONNECTIONS   56   © 1991 AIMS Education Foundation

Part 1

 Question - How will electricity flow in the circuit shown below?

 Prediction - Look at the diagram below and guess what will happen.

      A. The bulbs will light when the switch is on (closed).
      B. The bulbs will light when the switch is off (open).
      C. The bulbs will not light at all.
      D. Other _____

 To do - Build the parallel circuit shown below.

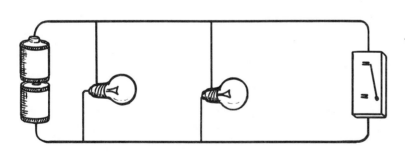

Now turn the switch on and off.

 Results - What happened?

_____

_____

 Conclusion - How can you explain the results?

_____

_____

Part 2

How does the location of the switch affect the flow of electricity?

Build these circuits. Which bulbs will light when the switch is on?

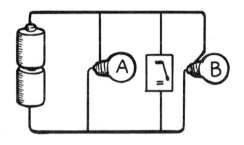

I think _____

because _____

_____

Results - _____

_____

I think _____

because _____

_____

Results - _____

_____

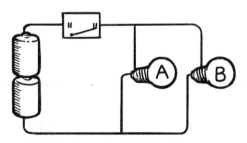

I think _____

because _____

_____

Results - _____

_____

Conclusions - How can you explain the results?

_____

_____

_____

_____

58

Put Your Name In Lights

Topic Area
Electric circuits - Morse code

Introductory Statement
Students will build a telegraph and send messages using Morse code.

Math
Problem solving
Patterning

Science
Observing
Classifying

Materials
Per group:
D cell
miniature Christmas light or bulb and holder
10-15 cm wires
switch
tape

Key Question
How can you build a device that will transmit messages using Morse code?

Background Information
See fact sheet on Samuel Morse.

Management
1. This lesson works best with groups of two.
2. The fact pages about Samuel Morse can be used to introduce this lesson.
3. This lesson is designed to follow the lessons on circuits and switches. The students should be able to build a simple circuit with a switch and bulb to act as a telegraph. If not, you may want to have a sample circuit built ahead of time to show them.
4. This activity can be used as part of a learning center.

Procedure
1. Review the fact sheet about Samuel Morse and discuss how the Morse code can be used to transmit messages using short and long flashes of light (dots and dashes).
2. Discuss the *Key Question:* "How can you build a device that will transmit messages by code?"
3. Challenge students to build a circuit that will act as a telegraph and enable them to send messages to each other in Morse code.
4. Pass out the materials and activity sheets, and have each group build a telegraph. Students use the activity sheet to send each other messages.

Discussion
1. How does your telegraph work?
2. How is the telegraph you built different from real telegraphs?

3. Why aren't telegraphs used widely today?
4. What devices have replaced the telegraph for communicating over long distances.

Extensions
1. Investigate other coding systems.
2. Encourage students to devise their own codes.
3. Have students build telegraphs that use a buzzer instead of a bulb.
4. Have students research and build telegraphs that are more like real telegraphs.

Curriculum Correlations
Art: Make a code using flags.
Social studies: Research other inventions that came on the scene about the same time as the telegraph. Study the history of the *Pony Express* and how the telegraph made it obsolete.

Put Your Name in Lights

International Morse Code -- --- •-• ••• •   -•-• --- -•• •

ALPHABET		NUMERALS	PUNCTUATION AND OTHER SIGNS
A •–	N –•	1 •––––	period •–•–•–
B –•••	O –––	2 ••–––	SOS •••–––•••
C –•–•	P •––•	3 •••––	end of message •–•–•
D –••	Q ––•–	4 ••••–	start –•–
E •	R •–•	5 •••••	understand •–•
F ••–•	S •••	6 –••••	question mark ••––••
G ––•	T –	7 ––•••	error ••••••••
H ••••	U ••–	8 –––••	
I ••	V •••–	9 ––––•	
J •–––	W •––	0 –––––	
K –•–	X –••–		
L •–••	Y –•––		
M ––	Z ––••		

1. Build a circuit that will allow you to send a Morse code message.

2. Write your name in Morse code. _____
   Send your name to your partner using your circuit.

3. Write a sentence in Morse code below and send it to your partner.

   _____
   _____
   _____
   _____

4. Decode your partner's message and write it in the space below.

   _____
   _____
   _____
   _____

The Electromagnetic Connection

Topic Area
Electromagnetism

Introductory Statement
Students will discover the relationship between electricity and magnetism.

Science
Observing
Drawing conclusions

Materials
Per group:
　　20 cm wire with ends stripped
　　D cell
　　magnetic compass
　　magnet

Key Question
What is the relationship between electricity and magnetism?

Background Information
One of the key discoveries in the history of science was made in 1820 when the Danish physicist Hans Christian Oersted accidentally discovered that an electric current in a wire deflected the magnetic needle of a nearby compass. This discovery led to the realization that electricity and magnetism are related. Scientists later discovered that electricity and magnetism are simply two aspects of the same fundamental electromagnetic force.

Oersted's discovery paved the way for the invention of electromagnets, electric motors, electric generators, and other devices that have radically changed the world in which we live. These devices are based on two fundamental principles: 1. moving electric charges create a magnetic field 2. moving magnetic fields create electric fields.

Management
1. Students should work in groups of three or four.
2. Any magnetic compass will work for this activity. Inexpensive compasses are available from toy stores.
3. This activity doesn't take much time and can be done in conjunction with *Make a Galvanometer.*

Procedure
1. Discuss the *Key Question:* "What is the relationship between electricty and magnetism?"
2. Pass out a compass to each group.
3. Have students place the compass on a flat surface and rotate its base. The needle will continue to point in the same direction because it is affected by the earth's magnetic field. Discuss this and have students write their explanations in the space provided.
4. Distribute a magnet to each group and have them bring it near the compass. The needle will be deflected by the magnet. Have students write their observations in the space provided.
5. Distribute a D cell and wire to each group. Connect the wire to the terminals of the cell and bring the wire near the compass needle. It will be deflected, proving that an electric current creates a magnetic field. Have students write their observations in the space provided. It is important to note that a current is present in the wire when it is connected to the terminals of the cell, even though it is not directly observable without seeing its effects on a compass.
6. Have students disconnect the wire and hold it next the compass. The needle will not be deflected. Students write their observations in the space provided.
7. Discuss the results of this activity and have students write their conclusions at the bottom of the sheet.

Discussion
1. What happens when the compass is placed on a flat surface and its base rotated? [the needle contiues to point in the same direction]
2. Why does this happen? [the needle is aligning itself with the earth's magnetic field]
3. What happens when a magnet is brought near the compass? [the needle is deflected]
4. Why does this happen? [when the magnet is near the compass, its magnetic field is stronger than the earth's magnetic field and it deflects the needle]
5. What happens when the wire connected to the D cell is brought near the compass? [the needle is deflected]
6. What does this prove? [an electric current produces a magnetic field]

Extensions
1. Try different lengths of wire and see if there is a difference.
2. Reverse the cell and note the difference.

Curriculum Correlations
Social studies: Have students research the role Oersted's discovery played in the history of electricity.
Science: Have students study how electric generators and electric motors work and relate this to Oersted's discovery.

The Electromagnetic Connection

What is the relationship between electricity and magnetism?

Find out!

You will need
    a magnetic compass
    a magnet
    a D cell
    20 cm wire with ends stripped

1.   Place the compass flat on your desk and rotate its base. What *do* you notice? Can you explain why the compass needle always points in the same direction? _____

_____

2.   Bring a magnet close to the compass. What happens? _____

_____

3.   Connect the wire to the terminals of the D cell. Now bring the wire close to the compass. What happens? _____

_____

4.   Disconnect the wire from the D cell. Bring the wire close to the compass again. What happens?_____

_____

What would this lead you to conclude?_____

_____

_____

Make a Galvanometer

Topic Area
Galvanometers

Introductory Statement
Students will construct a galvanometer, a device that detects small amounts of electric current.

Science
Observing
Drawing conclusions

Materials
Per group:
50 cm of insulated wire with ends stripped
D cell
magnetic compass

Key Question
What is a galvanometer?

Background Information
When a current flows through a wire, it creates a magnetic field which surrounds the wire. The polarity of this magnetic field depends on the direction of the current in the wire. The strength of the magnetic field depends on the amount of current flowing through the wire. For any set amount of current, the magnetic field around a wire can be strengthened by coiling the wire. The more coils a wire has, the stronger the magnetic field produced by a given current.

Johann Schweigger, a German physicist, built the first galvanometer shortly after Oersted's discovery of the connection between electricity and magnetism. *A galvanometer is a device that detects and measures small electric currents.* Schweigger's galvanometer consisted of a magnetized needle surrounded by a coil of wire. When an electric current was present in the coil, it created a magnetic field that deflected the needle. When the current to the coil was reversed, the needle was deflected in the opposite direction. Modern galvanometers are similar to the galvanometer built by Schweigger and the one made in this lesson.

Management
1. Students should be in groups of three or four.
2. Any magnetic compass will work for this activity. Inexpensive compasses are available from toy stores.
3. This activity can be done on the same day as *The Electromagnetic Connection.*

Procedure
1. Discuss the *Key Question:* "What is a galvanometer?"
2. Distribute materials to each group.
3. Have students build a galvanometer following the instructions on the activity sheet.
4. Connect the D cell to the galvanometer and observe what happens. Record the observations.
5. Reverse the D cell and connect it to the galvanometer once more. Observe what happens and record observations.
6. Discuss the results and write conclusions at the bottom of the activity sheet.

Discussion
1. What happens when the D cell is attached to the galvanometer? [the compass needle is deflected]
2. Why does this happen? [the current in the coil of wire creates a magnetic field that interacts with the magnetic field of the compass]
3. What happens when the D cell is reversed? [the needle is deflected in the opposite direction]
4. What does this prove? [the direction of the current determines the polarity of the magnetic field]

Extensions
1. Use different gauges or lengths of wire for the galvanometer.
2. Try more than one cell (or older cells) and note the difference.

Make a Galvanometer!

What is a galvanometer?

It is an instrument which detects the presence of small amounts of electric current.

In 1820 a Danish scientist named Hans Christian Oersted discovered accidentally that whenever an electric current flows through a wire, a magnetic field is created. A few months later, a German scientist named Johann Schweigger built the first simple galvanometer.

To build your own galvanometer, you will need

    50 cm insulated wire with ends stripped

    a magnetic compass

    a D cell

1. Wrap the wire around the compass in a north-south orientation, leaving about 10 cm free at each end.

2. Align the compass so the needle points north.

3. Attach the ends of the wire to the terminals of the D cell.

What happens? _____

Reverse the D cell and attach the ends of the wires again.
What happens? _____

Conclusions _____

_____

_____

How to Make An Electric Motor

Topic Area
Electric motors

Introductory Statement
Students will build a simple electric motor.

Math
Measuring

Science
Observing
Controlling variables
Generalizing and applying

Materials
Per group:
2 D cells
2 jumbo (5 cm long) metal paper clips
modeling clay
3 ring magnets
2 20-30 cm wires with ends stripped
55 cm piece of 18-22 gauge magnet wire (copper
 wire coated with enamel)
35 mm film canister
masking tape
ruler
scissors

Key Question
How can we build an electric motor?

Background Information
An electric motor is a machine that changes electrical energy into mechanical energy. Electric motors are based on three principles: electric currents produce magnetic fields; the direction of the current determines the polarity of the magnetic field produced; and like magnetic poles repel while unlike poles attract.

A simple, direct-current electric motor consists of a coil of wire connected to a freely rotating shaft. The coil becomes an electromagnet when current goes through the wire. This coil and shaft assembly, called the *armature*, is positioned between two stationary permanent magnets with the north pole of one magnet and the south pole of the other magnet facing the amature. As current passes through the armature, it creates a magnetic field. When the armature's north pole is near the north pole of the stationary magnet, the armature is repelled and makes a half turn, approaching the south pole of the other permanent magnet to which it is attracted. Just as the armature reaches the south pole, the current to the armature is reversed (by a part called the *commutator*). This reversal of current causes the armature's north pole to become a south pole. Once again, two like poles are next to each other and the armature is repelled, making another half rotation. This process continues as long as current is present in the armature.

The motor built in this activity is not as complex as the one described above. It has no commutator to reverse the direction of the current and will not usually start unless its armature (coil) is given a spin. The coil only has current going through it half the time.

Here is how this motor works. As mentioned, the coil is given a spin. As the bottom half of the coil approaches the permanent magnet, the uninsulated part of its arms make electrical contact with the paper clips. This allows a current to flow through the coil making it an electromagnet. At this time the two magnets (electromagnet and permanent) will have the same or opposite polarity. If they have opposite polarity, they will be attracted to one another and the coil will move down toward the magnet with increased speed. If they have the same polarity, the coil and magnet will repel one another. If the coil is moving slowly, it may reverse its course, but if it has enough momentum to reach the magnet, the repulsion will push it upward (in the same direction) to start its next cycle. When the coil swings around, the current is interrupted, stopping the magnetic field for half a turn. When the current flows through the coil again, the two magnetic poles either repel or attract each other once more. After the coil starts spinning, momentum carries it through the part of its cycle when there is no current.

Management
1. Building an electric motor that works can be a frustrating experience. It may take much patience and repeated tinkering. It is highly advisable that the teacher build a working motor before doing this activity with students. This will provide an appreciation for the task and a working model for students to examine.
2. Students should work in groups of two to four.
3. This is an open-ended activity which allows many opportunities for discovery.
4. Be sure to use the type of wire specified in the materials list. Enameled wire is commonly called magnet wire; it is available from electronics stores and shops that repair electric motors.
5. Empty 35 mm film canisters can be obtained free from one-hour photo-developing businesses.

Procedure
1. Discuss the *Key Question:* "How can we build an electric motor?"
2. Distribute activity sheets and materials.
3. Make the coil by wrapping the enameled wire around the film canister five times, leaving 4 cm free at each end. Remove canister and twist the ends around the coil twice to hold it together. Then bend the ends so that they are at right angles to the coil, directly opposite each other (see illustration on

student sheet). Scrape the insulation from the <u>bottom half</u> of these two arms (see illustration). Make the coil as symmetrical and well-balanced as possible.

4. Set up the motor according to the diagram on the first activity sheet. Start the motor by giving the coil a spin. If the coil doesn't continue spinning, have students check the list on the second activity sheet.

5. Challenge students to find a way to reverse the direction the coil spins or get the coil to spin faster.

Discussion
1. Why does the coil spin? [its magnetic field is repelled or attracted by the magnetic field of the ring magnets]
2. Why must the coil be properly balanced? [an unbalanced coil does not spin as easily as a balanced one and will not keep spinning]
3. How could you increase the speed of the motor? [increase the number of cells used and/or increase the length of wire and number of turns in your coil]
4. Where are electric motors used?

Extensions
1. Take apart an old electric motor and see if you can identify its parts.
2. Have students find all the electric motors in the classroom or in their homes.

Curriculum Correlations
Social studies: Research the history of the electric motor.

HOW TO MAKE AN ELECTRIC MOTOR

Materials:

2 D cells	2 jumbo paper clips	clay
3 ring magnets	55 cm magnet wire	2 short wires
masking tape	35 mm film canister	ruler and scissors

1. Make your coil by wrapping the magnet wire tightly around the film canister. Leave 4 cm of wire free at each end. Twist these two ends around the coil twice to hold the coil together. Bend the ends away from the coil directly opposite each other as shown below.

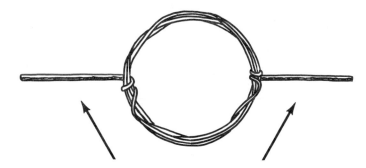

2. Use the scissors to scrape the enamel from the bottom half of each arm as shown above.

3. Bend the paper clips as shown below.

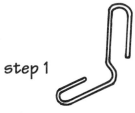

step 1

step 2

4. Set up the circuit as pictured and give the coil a spin. If it keeps going, you've built a working electric motor!

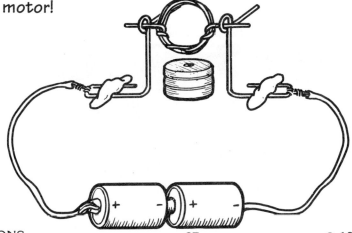

ELECTRICAL CONNECTIONS
67
© 1991 AIMS Education Foundation

If your motor does not work, check the following:

1. Your motor should be set up on a level surface.

2. Make sure your coil is as well balanced as possible. It should spin without wobbling.

3. Try spinning your coil in both directions. It may work in one direction and not the other.

4. Make sure that the wires are making good electrical contact with the battery terminals and the paper clips.

5. Try flipping the magnets over so that the opposite pole is facing the coil.

6. Make sure the enamel is completely scraped off the bottom half of each arm. The coil needs to make good electrical contact for half of each rotation.

7. Check the clearance between the bottom of the coil and the magnets. It should be about one cm.

8. Make sure that the two loops in the paper clips are the same height. The arms of the coil need to be level to allow the coil to spin freely. Adjust with clay.

When your motor is working, here are some challenges.

1. Make your coil spin in both directions.

2. Try to make your coil spin faster.

3. Put a switch in your circuit. It is a real challenge to get your motor to start by simply closing the switch.

ELECTROMAGNETISM

Whenever an electric current goes through a wire, a magnetic field is created around the wire. Electricity and magnetism are related; an electric current produces a magnetic field, and a change in a magnetic field can produce an electric current. When current goes through a coiled wire, the magnetic field is strengthened because each coil acts like a separate magnet.

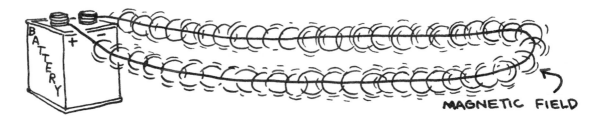

MAGNETIC FIELD

The strength of an electromagnet can be increased in several ways. The number of coils can be increased. The voltage of the current going through the wire can be increased. Using a metal core, such as a nail or a bolt, will also increase the strength of the electromagnet. The magnetic field produced by the current in the coils induces a magnetic field in the iron core.

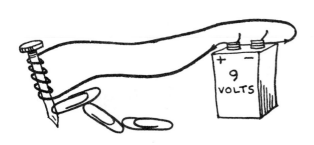

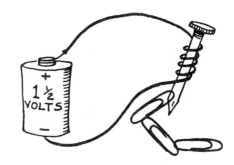

Electromagnets are an integral part of many common devices such as telephones, electric motors, generators, televisions, and door bells.

Electromagnets

Topic Area
Electromagnets

Introductory Statement
Students will experiment with electromagnets by manipulating several variables. Through these activities students should discover how an electromagnet works and, ultimately, how to make it more efficient.

Math
Computing
Averaging
Graphing
Tabulating
Measuring
   diameter
   length
   mass
   area of a circle

Science
Reporting data
Collecting data
Identifying and controlling
   variables
Making and testing
   hypotheses
Interpreting data

Key Questions (one per investigation):
Build a Better Magnet. - How does neatness affect the power of the magnet?

Core Size - How will changing the diameter of the bolt affect the amount of weight a magnet can hold?

Wire Wraps - How does changing the number of times the wire is wrapped around the bolt affect the holding ability of the magnet?

Wire Gauge - How will changing the thickness of the wire change the magnet's strength?

Stretching the Magnet - How does the holding ability of the magnet change if the same number of wraps are used but spread out over a longer bolt?

Power Shortage - What happens to the strength of the magnet when the voltage is decreased?

Background Information
See *Electromagnetism* fact sheet.

As your students will discover, the construction of an electromagnet is quite simple; for it to be efficient, however, materials and procedures must be followed carefully. In these investigations, several terms are used which may not be common knowledge:

   core size - diameter of the bolt exclusive of the head

   insulation - plastic coating on the wire

   wire strippers - a pliers-like tool designed to take the plastic coating off the outside of the wire without damaging the wire itself

   wire gauge - the number denoting the thickness of the wire, the higher the number, the thinner the wire - normal bell wire is 18-20 gauge

   wraps - the number of times a wire is wrapped around the bolt that is going to become the electromagnet.

Management
1. This series of activities can take place over a period of several weeks. The first three activity sheets contain basic information on electromagnets. Then, each of the other activity tests one variable and can be done on a different day.
2. Students should work in groups of three or four.
3. The activities work best if you can use the equipment shown on the *Basic Set-up* page. If you do not have access to a variable transformer or balance, two alternatives are shown on the *Alternate Set-ups* page.
4. These activities are open-ended; students should be allowed plenty of freedom to explore.
5. It is not necessary to do all of the activities included here for students to get a good understanding of electromagnets. Pick activities that are appropriate for your students.
6. The culminating activity is a contest and does not have a student sheet.

Procedure
Learning about electromagnets:

Distribute materials for students to make one type of basic set-up. Use activity sheets titled *Electromagnets, Basic Set-up,* and *Alternate Set-ups* to discuss with students what is happening. During the discussion, guide students to understand and use the terminology given above in *Background Information.*

When using the balance to test the strength of the electromagnet, use the following steps:
1. Estimate the amount of mass the magnet will hold and load that amount of mass in the balance pan.
2. While holding the magnet beneath the opposite balance pan, pull the pan down until it touches the magnet.
3. Turn on the transformer or connect the batteries.
4. Release the scale pan. If the magnet holds the pan down for two to three seconds, shut off the transformer to prevent overheating. If the magnet does not hold, turn off the transformer immediately.
5. If necessary, revise the estimate, add or remove gram masses as needed, and retest the electromagnet.

When using the spring scale to test the strength of the electromagnet use the following steps:
1. Estimate the force (newtons) or mass (grams) that the electromagnet will hold and record estimate.
2. Tape an iron washer to the hook of the spring scale and hold it over the electromagnet.
3. Attach the electromagnet to the battery and touch it to the washer on the spring scale.

4. Hold the electromagnet steady while pulling away with the spring scale. Note and record the reading on the scale when the magnet pulls free. Disconnect the battery to prevent drain.

When using a nail and paper clips, use the following steps:
1. Estimate and record the number of paper clips the electromagnet will hold.
2. Connect the battery to the electromagnet and touch the electromagnet to a pile of paper clips. Lift the electromagnet and count the number of paper clips held.
3. Disconnect the battery to prevent drain, and record what happens.

Below are some general instructions that apply to the rest of the activities:
1. Students are asked to test a different variable in each of the other investigations. The variable is identified in the key question.
2. Students should be asked to predict or hypothesize before doing each activity.
3. Students should keep accurate records of their research.

The culminating activity for this series is a contest in which students design an electromagnet using any of the materials available. The goal of the contest is to build the strongest possible electromagnet using knowledge about the different variables gained in these activities.

Extensions
1. Encourage students to show their results in a variety of ways: line graphs, circle graphs, demonstrations, written reports, etc.
2. Have students list identified variables and set up additional investigations to determine the effect of changing two variables instead of only one.
3. Have students research various devices that use electromagnets, such as electric motors, electrical generators, or cranes used to move scrap iron.
4. Build models of devices that use electromagnets.

Electromagnets

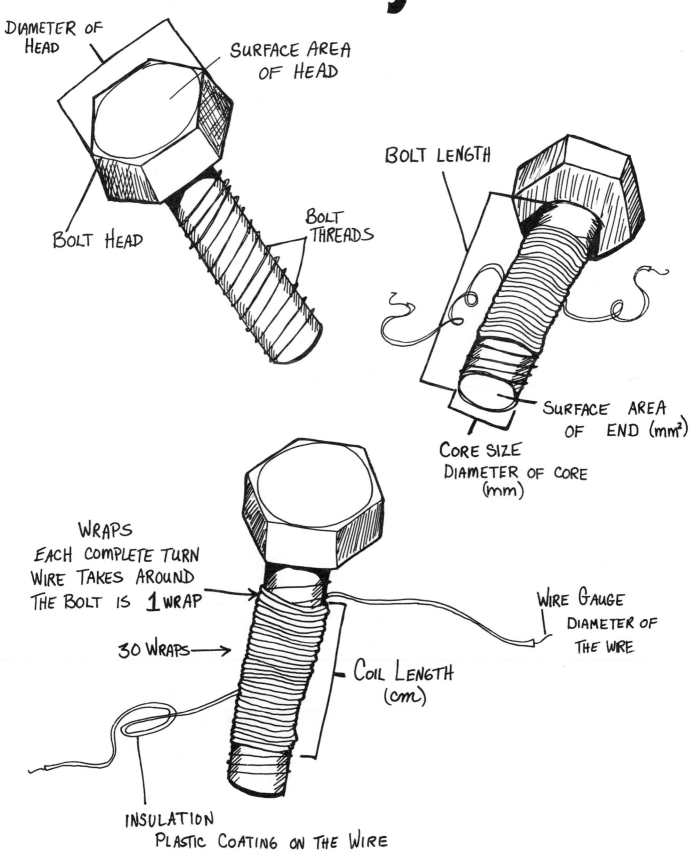

DIAMETER OF HEAD

SURFACE AREA OF HEAD

BOLT HEAD

BOLT THREADS

BOLT LENGTH

SURFACE AREA OF END (mm²)

CORE SIZE DIAMETER OF CORE (mm)

WRAPS
EACH COMPLETE TURN WIRE TAKES AROUND THE BOLT IS **1** WRAP

30 WRAPS →

COIL LENGTH (cm)

WIRE GAUGE DIAMETER OF THE WIRE

INSULATION
PLASTIC COATING ON THE WIRE

Basic Set-up

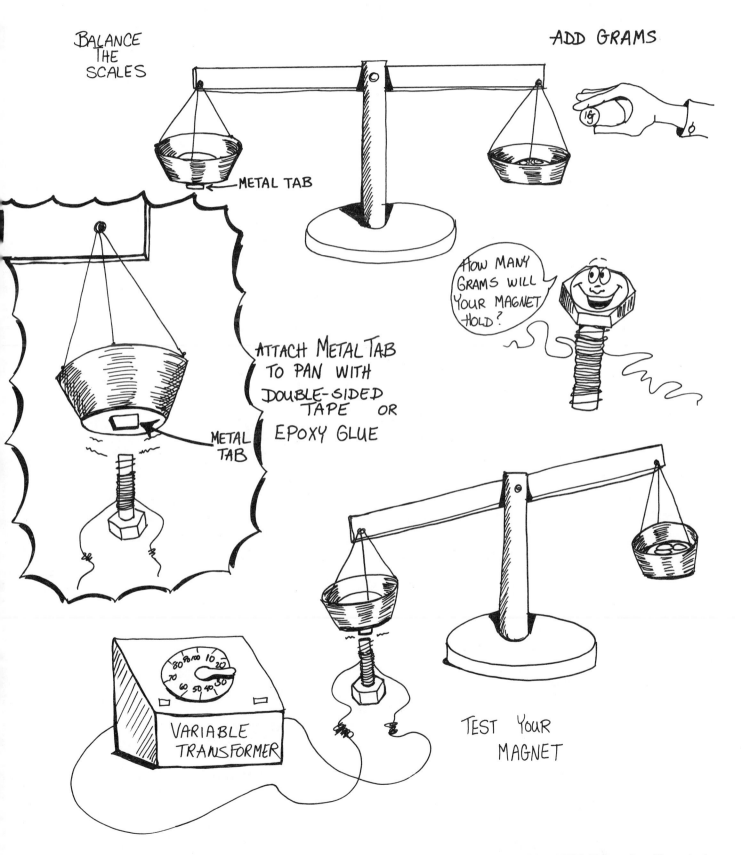

Alternate Set-ups

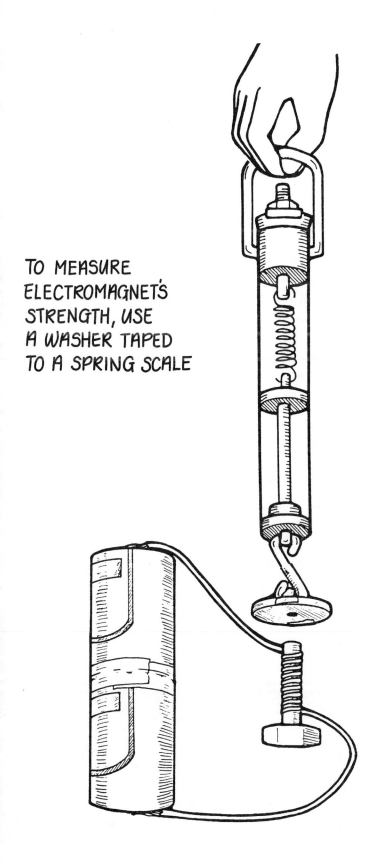

TO MEASURE
ELECTROMAGNET'S
STRENGTH, USE
A WASHER TAPED
TO A SPRING SCALE

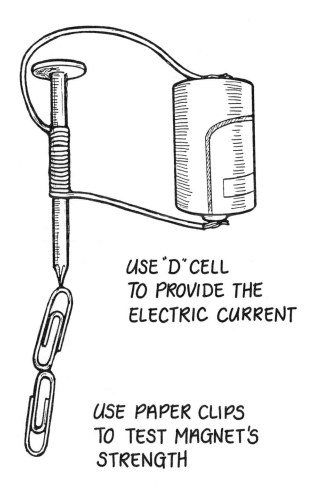

USE NAILS FOR CORES.

USE "D" CELL
TO PROVIDE THE
ELECTRIC CURRENT

USE PAPER CLIPS
TO TEST MAGNET'S
STRENGTH

Build a Better Magnet

How Does Neatness Affect the Strength of the Magnet?

	MESSY	NEAT	MESSY	NEAT	MESSY	NEAT	MESSY	NEAT	MESSY	NEAT
1										
2										
3										
4										
5										
TOTAL										
AVERAGE										
	Magnet **1**		Magnet **2**		Magnet **3**		Magnet **4**		Magnet **5**	
WRAPS										
WIRE DIAMETER										
COIL LENGTH										
WIRE GAUGE										
SURFACE AREA OF END										

TEST NUMBER

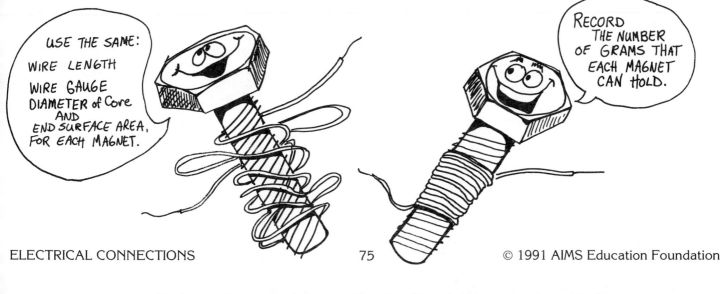

USE THE SAME:
WIRE LENGTH
WIRE GAUGE
DIAMETER of Core
AND
END SURFACE AREA,
FOR EACH MAGNET.

RECORD THE NUMBER OF GRAMS THAT EACH MAGNET CAN HOLD.

Core Size

How will changing the diameter of the bolt affect the amount of weight a magnet can hold?

Core Diameter

Test Number	5mm	6mm	7mm	8mm	9mm	10mm	11mm	17mm
1								
2								
3								
4								
5								
TOTAL								
AVERAGE								
WRAPS								
COIL LENGTH								
WIRE GAUGE								
SURFACE AREA OF END								

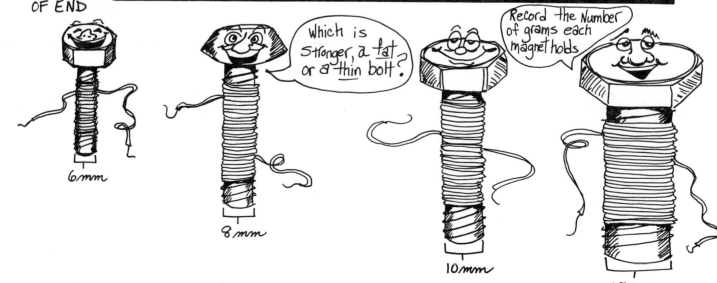

Which is stronger, a _fat_ or a _thin_ bolt?

Record the number of grams each magnet holds

6mm

8mm

10mm

17mm

Wire Wraps

How Does Changing the Number of Times the Wire is Wrapped Around the Bolt Affect the Holding Ability of the Magnet?

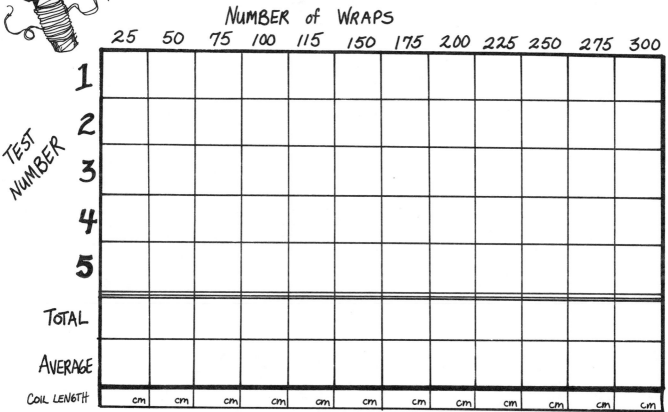

NUMBER of WRAPS

TEST NUMBER	25	50	75	100	115	150	175	200	225	250	275	300
1												
2												
3												
4												
5												
TOTAL												
AVERAGE												
COIL LENGTH	cm	cm	cm	cm	cm	cm	cm	cm	cm	cm	cm	cm

Record the number of grams the magnet was able to hold on each try.

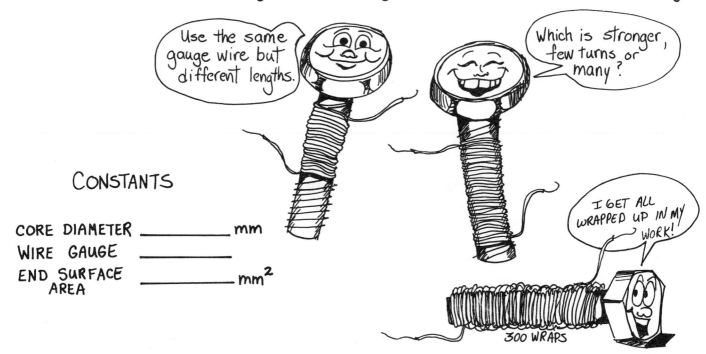

Use the same gauge wire but different lengths.

Which is stronger, few turns or many?

I GET ALL WRAPPED UP IN MY WORK!

300 WRAPS

CONSTANTS

CORE DIAMETER _____ mm

WIRE GAUGE _____

END SURFACE AREA _____ mm²

Wire Gauge

HOW WILL CHANGING THE THICKNESS OF THE WIRE CHANGE THE MAGNET'S STRENGTH?

WIRE GAUGE → DIAMETER OF THE WIRE

	10	12	14	16	18	20	22	24	26	28	52		
1													
2													
3													
4													
5													
TOTAL													
AVERAGE													
COIL LENGTH	cm	cm	cm	cm	cm	cm	cm	cm	cm	cm	cm	cm	cm

TEST NUMBER

Record the number of grams each magnet holds.

Use the same number of wraps and the same diameter bolt.

Does Thinner or Thicker Wire Make a Better Magnet?

CONSTANTS

WRAPS _____

CORE DIAMETER _____

END SURFACE AREA _____

Stretching the Magnet

HOW DOES THE HOLDING ABILITY OF THE MAGNET CHANGE IF THE SAME NUMBER OF WRAPS ARE USED, BUT SPREAD OUT OVER A LONGER BOLT?

LENGTH OF COIL (cm)

	2	3	4	5	6	7	8	9	10		
1											
2											
3											
4											
5											
TOTAL											
AVERAGE											

CONSTANTS

WRAPS _____

CORE DIAMETER _____ mm

WIRE GAUGE _____

END SURFACE _____ mm²
AREA

Use the SAME Number of turns, Wire gauge, and bolt diameter.

Power Shortage

WHAT HAPPENS TO THE STRENGTH OF A MAGNET
WHEN THE VOLTAGE IS DECREASED ?

Record the number of grams the magnet holds at different power levels.

VOLTAGE					
1					
2					
3					
4					
5					
TOTAL					
AVERAGE					

Use a previously constructed magnet. FIND YOUR BEST ONE!

CONSTANTS

WRAPS _____

CORE DIAMETER _____ mm

COIL LENGTH _____ cm

WIRE GAUGE _____

END SURFACE AREA _____ mm²

Biographies

Here are some ways to use these biography fact sheets.

1.   Divide the class into three groups. Give each group the biography on one person. Students read the factual information and create a short skit with props and narrator. Extras could include making posters to advertise the "events."

2.   Let each student choose one person's biography and tell that person's story (in oral or written form) from the point of view of another person or an animal. It could even be a television (or radio!) series.

3.   Have students make scrapbooks containing the biography fact sheets plus other reports and clippings related to the person or persons chosen.

4.   Each student might choose one inventor, research that person, and make other pictures with captions besides those provided.

5.   Discuss the impact of the inventions of these three persons. Take a class or school survey to determine what students think are the major inventions during all time or during any given time period like the twentieth century.

6.   These inventors have been featured because they are already well-known to most students. Research others, especially women and those of minority ethnic groups.

7.   Challenge students to go through one day without using something one of these three men invented or improved upon.

Benjamin Franklin - Page 1

Benjamin Franklin was born on January 17, 1706. He was the tenth son of seventeen children. His father was a soapmaker and a candlemaker.

At twelve, he became an apprentice printer. This led to printing a newspaper, the paper currency for several colonies, and Poor Richard's Almanac which is a collection of wise sayings.

His love of books led him to create the first subscription library in America. Members contributed money which was used to purchase books. These books were then loaned to the members free of charge. It allowed people access to many books.

He brought about many improvements in Philadelphia. Alarmed by the large number of homes and businesses lost to fire, Franklin established a "volunteer" fire department. He also organized the first hospital in America.

Benjamin Franklin - Page 2

He made a kite that he flew during a thunderstorm. The lightning struck a wire on the kite, travelled down the string, and caused a spark on the key. In 1752 this experiment led to the invention of the lightning rod and proved that lightning is actually electricity.

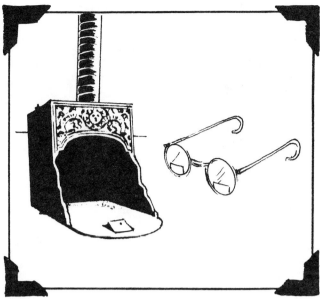

Other inventions included bifocal glasses and the Franklin stove. Since people used stoves for heating their homes, it was important that the Franklin stove gave off more heat than regular stoves.

Franklin is the only American to have signed all four major documents: the Declaration of Independence, the Constitution, the Treaty of Alliance with France, and the Treaty of Peace with Great Britain.

Benjamin Franklin was a talented man. He served his nation as a statesman, scientist, and community servant.

Samuel Morse

Samuel Morse was born on April 27, 1791 in Massachusetts. His interest in art plus his hard work led to success both as an artist and also an art teacher.

While sailing home from Europe in 1832, Morse learned that electricity could be sent instantly over any length of wire. This was the beginning of his quest to invent the telegraph.

Morse tried one dramatic demonstration by laying wire under water. Crowds came to see the telegraph work. Unfortunately, a ship's anchor pulled up the wire and cut it. The disappointed crowd left, calling the whole thing a hoax.

Finally, with a grant of money from Congress, Morse succeeded. In 1844, Morse strung a wire from the Supreme Court Building in Washington, D.C., to Baltimore, Maryland. He sent the now famous message, "What hath God wrought!" Morse won great fame and wealth from his invention. He died in 1872.

Thomas Edison - Page 1

Thomas Edison was born in Ohio on February 11, 1847. He began school at the age of seven. His schooling lasted only three months because his teachers were angry that he asked too many unusual questions. From then on, Edison's mother, a teacher, taught him at home.

When Edison was 12, he took a job selling newspapers on board the Grand Trunk Railway. In his spare time, he would do experiments in the baggage car. One day, an experiment caught fire. He was physically kicked off the train, chemicals and all.

His favorite invention was the phonograph. He invented it in 1877. The first words ever recorded on the machine were, "Mary had a little lamb."

In addition to his own inventions, including a vote-counting machine, he improved upon the inventions of others: the telegraph, the typewriter, and stock ticker systems.

Thomas Edison - Page 2

Edison was nearly deaf. He believed that he lost his hearing when a well-meaning conductor tried to help him board a moving train by pulling him by his ears. Edison could have had an operation to cure his deafness, but he did not want to because he found it easier to concentrate when it was quiet.

In 1879, while living in Menlo Park, New Jersey, Edison worked on perfecting the electric light. He spent two years searching for the proper filament. Finally, after over 7,000 tries, he successfully invented the electric light bulb.

Even after he was 80 years old, Edison was busy creating and improving inventions. He began research on synthetic rubber. In 1931, while working in his laboratory, he collapsed and died.

Thomas Edison was one of the greatest inventors in the history of our country. He patented over 1,093 inventions in his lifetime. He has become known world-wide as the "Wizard of Menlo Park."

Electricity Time Line

Topic Area
History of electricity

Introductory Statement
Students will construct a time line of some major events in the history of electricity.

Math
Sequencing
Measuring
Estimating

Science
Classifying
Collecting data
Organizing data

Materials:
Per group of four:
1 copy of date page
3 copies of inventor page
clear tape
crayons
scissors
1 2-3 m piece of yarn
12 20-30 cm pieces of yarn
meter stick or tape (*optional*)

Per student:
Charging in Time fact sheets

Key Question
How did discoveries about electricity develop over a period of time?

Background Information
See fact sheets, *Charging In Time.*

Management
1. Students should work in groups of four.
2. Hang the long piece of yarn near where each group will meet. You may wish to make this a math activity. With younger students, hang the 1750 sign and have them add a sign every __ cm. Older students may enjoy measuring the total length and dividing by the number of signs.

Procedure
1. Tell students that they are going to construct a time line which will show the dates of some electrical inventions and discoveries.
2. Put students in groups of four. Distribute *Charging in Time* fact sheets and have students read them.
3. Distribute three copies of the inventor page to each group or enough for each student to get three cards.
4. Each person selects three of the inventions or discoveries listed on the fact sheets. Summarize the information and/or draw the inventions.

5. Pass out a copy of the date page to each group. Have students cut along the solid lines and fold each piece along the dashed line. Students place the dates on the yarn so that they are equally spaced (they can use a meter stick/tape to do this) and tape or staple them in place.
6. Have each group hang their invention summary cards (using the short pieces of yarn) on their time line. Students should place the cards in the correct position by *interpolating* (estimating the distance between two points). For example, a card about Oersted's 1820 discovery of the relationship between electricity and magnetism would be placed between the 1800 and 1825 dates on the time line, but it would be much closer to 1825.
7. Have each group study their completed time line and interpret the data.
8. As a class, discuss the importance of various inventions.

Discussion
1. What information do you get from the time line?
2. How is this information similar to the information on the fact sheet?
3. How is this information different from the fact sheet?
4. What are some advantages of presenting this kind of information in the form of a time line?
5. What are the disadvantages?
6. Which period had the most inventions?
7. Why do you think that happened?

Extensions
1. Research other electrical inventions/discoveries and add them to the time line.
2. Make a time line that starts in more modern times and focuses on modern inventions that use electricity such as VCR's, CD players, fax machines, etc.
3. Make time lines for other areas of study.

Curriculum Correlations
Language arts: Write a news article or advertisement for one of the inventions on the time line.
Social studies: Find out more about some of the scientists or inventions on the time line.

Date

Inventor

Invention

Date

Inventor

Invention

Date

Inventor

Invention

Date

Inventor

Invention

1750	1750	1925	1925
1775	1775	1900	1900
1800	1800	1875	1875
1825	1825	1850	1850

CHARGING IN TIME

Many people have contributed to our understanding of electricity today. The ancient Greeks first discovered that amber rubbed with cloth would attract bits of straw and other light objects. This phenomenon, which was caused by static electricity, was known for over two thousand years before it was studied in any great depth. In the early 1600's William Gilbert, a physicist from England, was the first to study static electricity in a scientific way. He is credited with coining the word electricity, which comes from the Greek word for amber. It was more than 100 years later that research on electricity progressed much farther.

In the summer of 1752, Benjamin Franklin performed his famous kite experiment which proved that lightning was an electric phenomenon. Franklin was lucky not to have been killed, a fate which fell on some who tried to duplicate his experiment. The same year, he made the first lightning rod and placed it on the top of a house. When the lightning struck, it hit the rod and was short circuited to the ground, sparing the house.

In 1800, Alessandro Volta of Italy, made the first wet-cell battery which produced an electrical current. He placed zinc and silver discs in an acid solution and an electric current flowed through a wire which was connected to the discs.

In 1820, Hans Oersted from Denmark, discovered the connection between electricity and magnetism. He noticed that an electric current in a wire deflected a compass needle that was near by. He discovered that whenever an electric current flows through a wire a magnetic field is created. Oersted's discovery led John Schweigger to invent the first galvanometer, a device to detect electric currents, in 1821.

In 1821, Michael Faraday from Great Britain, invented the first basic electric motor. He placed a wire carrying an electric

current between the poles of a magnet. When the two magnetic fields met, they caused a force that made the wire turn around creating the first electric motor.

In 1823 W. Sturgeon, a scientist from Great Britain, made the first electromagnet by passing an electric current through a wire which was wrapped around an iron bar. The iron bar became a powerful magnet when an electric current was going through the wires wrapped around it.

In 1831 Michael Faraday invented the first transformer, a device which could change the voltage of an electric current. When a current with a low voltage entered the transformer, it was transformed into a current with a high voltage coming out.

In 1844, Samuel Morse successfully transmitted a message by magnetic telegraph. This invention allowed people to communicate over great distances.

In 1866, G. Leclanche from France, made the first dry-cell battery by combining different chemicals in a small round container. The dry-cell battery made it possible to have a convenient, easy-to-use source of power.

For the next few years, Thomas Edison was very busy inventing many different products. In 1877, he developed the first phonograph. Two years later, in 1879, he invented the first successful electric light bulb. It was a glass bulb which burned for only 13 1/2 hours. Luckily, a year before in 1878, J. Swan had developed a vacuum pump to remove the air from a bulb so the filament would not burn away.

In 1907, the electric vacuum cleaner and washing machine were invented which made house cleaning much easier.

It wasn't until 1910 that G. Claude, France, produced the first neon light. He passed an electric current through a neon gas tube which made the gas glow red.

In 1925, J. Baird from Scotland, demonstrated the first television set but it was many years later before it became available to many families.

When I Was Ten

Topic Area
History of electricity

Introductory Statement
Students will find out how daily living and the uses of electricity have changed through the years by interviewing older people.

Math
Sequencing
Calculating age

Science
Classifying
Organizing data
Reporting

Materials
Copies of activity sheets

Key Question
How have electrical inventions changed the way we live?

Background Information
Students (and adults) take the conveniences of modern life for granted. They do not stop to think that things like TV's, refrigerators, or calculators have not always been available and that their grandparents or other older people actually went through childhood with out these "necessities." This activity is designed to help students realize what important changes have come about through the use of devices that use electricity.

Management
1. This activity has three parts. *Part 1* includes a class discussion and an assignment for students to interview older people in their families or neighborhoods. *Part 2* is done after students have completed their interviews, perhaps several days later. *Part 3* enables students to calculate someone's age.
2. If most students do not have access to older people in their families or neighborhoods, adapt the activity by conducting interviews on the phone. Seniors might enjoy visiting the school to be interviewed. Planning the activity just before Thanksgiving or another family-oriented holiday might also help.
3. This activity is designed to focus on how life has changed because of modern electrical conveniences, but it certainly should not be limited to this focus. It might be good for today's students to hear seniors talk about how they spent their time as school-age children.
4. Two versions of *Part 2* are included. Pick the one more appropriate for your students.

Procedure
Part 1
1. Introduce the lesson by brainstorming activities students like. After a list has been generated, discuss which activities are directly or indirectly related to electricity. Many activities will be linked directly to electricity: watching television, listening to tapes, playing video games, etc. Others will be linked less directly: playing baseball involves the use of bats, balls, and gloves made in factories using electricity. Through this discussion students will become aware of the many ways electricity and electrical devices affect their lives.
2. Discuss the *Key Question*: "How have electrical inventions changed the way we live?" Ask students to imagine what life would be like without some of the modern conveniences like TV's, vacuum cleaners, telephones, etc.
3. Ask students how they think their great-grandparents or grandparents performed simple tasks like cleaning their house or cooking their food when they were ten. Ask students what they think their grandparents did for entertainment when they were young and how it was different from what school-age children do today. Tell the class that they will try to find the answers to these and other questions by interviewing older people.
4. Distribute an interview sheet to each student. Tell students that you would like them to interview a grandparent, great-grandparent, or other senior who was born before 1920. The interviews will focus on what their lives were like when they were ten.
5. Tell students that the questions listed on the interview sheet are to help them get started with their interviews. Encourage them to add questions of their own in the spaces provided. The back of the sheet can be used for information volunteered by the person interviewed or for additional questions.
6. Give the students a deadline for getting the interviews completed.

Part 2
1. After students have finished the interview process, have them share their findings.
2. Discuss some of the ways that the life of a ten-year-old was different in the childhood of the person interviewed.
3. Brainstorm a list of common electrical devices that were not available when the people interviewed were younger.
4. Discuss the differences these devices have made in our life-styles.

5. Have students try to imagine living in a world without modern electrical conveniences.
6. Have students pick three electric devices and write what they would use if they didn't have that device.
7. Have students write a paragraph describing how their lives would be different without electricity.

Part 3
1. Have them calculate their age and date of birth using the steps outlined.
2. Have students calculate the age of their senior friend using the information from the interview.

Discussion
1. How have electrical devices changed the way we live?
2. Are all of these changes for the better?
3. Would you have liked to have been a child during the time your grandparents were growing up? Why or why not?
4. What electrical devices do you feel you could live without?
5. What electrical devices do you feel you couldn't live without?

Extensions
1. Make a time line that shows some of the major electrical inventions from the time your grandparents were 10 up to the present.
2. Find some inventions that are less than 10 years old and learn more about them.
3. Try to imagine how your life will be different in 50 years because of new inventions and write about it.

Curriculum Correlations
Language Arts: Write a story about the childhood of your grandparents or whomever you interviewed.
Art: Make a collage that shows modern electrical devices. Draw pictures of what you think your home will look like in 50 years.

Home Link
Challenge students (and parents) to do without TV for one full day. Discuss the reactions in the students' homes.

Name _____

When I Was Ten

Part 1

Our class at school is studying electricity. We are trying to find out what a difference electricity has made in people's lives. We appreciate your willingness to help us.

1. What is your name? _____
2. When you were ten years old, did your home have electricity? _____
    _____
3. What did people do before they had electric lights at night? _____
    _____
4. How did you keep food cold? _____
    _____
5. How did you wash your clothes? _____
    _____
6. When you were ten years old, what did you do in your spare time?
    _____
7. Do you think electricity was a good invention ?_____
    _____
8. What is your date of birth? year_____month_____day _____
9. _____
    _____
10. _____
    _____
11. _____
    _____
12 _____
    _____

Thank you for talking with me.

_____Interviewer

Name_____

When I Was Ten

Electricity is a part of our lives. Although it is difficult to imagine what life would be like without our things that use electricity, let's think what we would do instead.

1. If I didn't have _____

    I would _____

    _____

2. If I didn't have _____

    I would _____

    _____

3. If I didn't have _____

    I would _____

    _____

Describe what you think your life would have been like without electricity.

_____

_____

_____

_____

_____

_____

_____

_____

_____

_____

_____

When I Was Ten

Part 2

Electricity is a part of our lives. Although it is difficult to imagine what life would be like without electricity, let's think what we would do instead.

If I didn't have. . .

I would. . .

If I didn't have. . .

I would. . .

If I didn't have. . .

I would. . .

This activity made me think about _____

_____

_____

_____

_____

96

When I Was Ten

Part 3

Here's how to find out how old someone is when you know the date of birth. Try it first with your own birth date.

Years	Months	Days
_____	_____	_____
_____	_____	_____
_____	_____	_____

1. Fill in today's date on these lines.
2. Fill in the date of birth on these lines.
3. Subtract, the days first.

(If you need to regroup, change 1 month to 30 days.)

4. Next, subtract the months. (If you need to regroup, change 1 year to 12 months.)
5. Then, subtract the years.
6. You now have your age: _____years, _____months, and _____days.

If you know a person's age, here is how to find out when a person was born. Again, try it with your own.

Years	Months	Days
_____	_____	_____
_____	_____	_____
_____	_____	_____

1. Fill in today's date here.
2. Fill in your age here.
3. Subtract, days first.

This is the date of birth:_____years, _____months, and _____days.

or _____ _____, _____
              month   day   year

Now find out your senior friend's exact age.

Years	Months	Days
_____	_____	_____
_____	_____	_____
_____	_____	_____

1. Fill in today's date on these lines.
2. Fill in the date of birth.
3. Subtract.

4. The person's age is:_____years, _____months, and _____days.

Problem-solving Activities
for Challenge and Assessment

The activities in this book are designed to be self-assessing. For example, you can tell whether or not students can build a circuit by having them do it. At the end of an electricity unit, however, you may wish to use different activities to see if students can apply what they have learned. You may also wish to provide them with challenges to stimulate further growth and creative thinking. If you use these activities for performance-based assessment, be sure all students being assessed have done successfully the investigations on which these activities are based.

1. Make a model of a light bulb. Use a six-volt lantern battery for the power source and a 10 cm length of 32 gauge nichrome wire (or a single strand of picture frame wire) for the filament. Coil the filament by wrapping it around a small nail and then removing the nail. Build a circuit containing the filament which has a switch. The filament gets extremely hot, so caution should be used.

2. Make a working flashlight using a toilet paper tube, a three-ounce paper cup, some aluminum foil, a flashlight bulb, and a D cell. The flashlight should have a switch.

3. Make a model of a village using boxes and construction paper. Install circuits and lights in each of the buildings in the village.

4. Devise a play in which students model what happens in an electric circuit. Students play the part of switches, lights, batteries, fuses, and electric charges (electrons).

5. Make a test circuit containing a light bulb to test the conductivity of different liquids. Some suggested liquids to test are salt water, vinegar, sugar water, and lemon juice.

6. Make a model of a fuse by taping a single strand of steel wool to a piece of tag board. Put the fuse in a circuit and vary the number of cells used to power the circuit. Try to make a fuse that will not burn with one or two cells in the circuit, but will burn with three cells.

The AIMS Program

AIMS is the acronym for "Activities Integrating Mathematics and Science." Such integration enriches learning and makes it meaningful and holistic. AIMS began as a project of Fresno Pacific College to integrate the study of mathematics and science in Grades K-9, but has since expanded to include language arts, social studies, and other disciplines.

AIMS is a continuing program of the non-profit AIMS Education Foundation. It had its inception in a National Science Foundation funded program whose purpose was to explore the effectiveness of integrating mathematics and science. The project directors in cooperation with eighty elementary classroom teachers devoted two years to a thorough field-testing of the results and implications of integration.

The approach met with such positive results that the decision was made to launch a program to create instructional materials incorporating this concept. Despite the fact that thoughtful educators have long recommended an integrative approach, very little appropriate material was available in 1981 when the project began. A series of writing projects have ensued and today the AIMS Education Foundation is committed to continue the creation of new integrated activities on a permanent basis.

The AIMS program is funded through the sale of this developing series of books and proceeds from the Foundation's endowment. All net income from book and poster sales flow into a trust fund administered by the AIMS Education Foundation. Use of these funds is restricted to support of research, development, publication of new materials, and partial scholarships for classroom teachers participating in writing and field testing teams. Writers donate all their rights to the Foundation to support its on-going program. No royalties are paid to the writers.

The rationale for integration lies in the fact that science, mathematics, language arts, social studies, etc., are integrally interwoven in the real world from which it follows that they should be similarly treated in the classroom where we are preparing students to live in that world. Teachers who use the AIMS program give enthusiastic endorsement to the effectiveness of this approach.

Science encompasses the art of questioning, investigating, hypothesizing, discovering and communicating. Mathematics is the language that provides clarity, objectivity, and understanding. The language arts provide us powerful tools of communication. Many of the major contemporary societal issues stem from advancements in science and must be studied in the context of the social sciences. Therefore, it is timely that all of us take seriously a more holistic mode of educating our students. This goal motivates all who are associated with the AIMS Program. We invite you to join us in this effort.

Meaningful integration of knowledge is a major recommendation coming from the nation's professional science and mathematics associations. The American Association for the Advancement of Science in *Science for All Americans* strongly recommends the integration of mathematics, science and technology. The National Council of Teachers of Mathematics places strong emphasis on applications of mathematics such as are found in science investigations. AIMS is fully aligned with these recommendations.

Extensive field testing of AIMS investigations confirms these beneficial results.

1. Mathematics becomes more meaningful, hence more useful, when it is applied to situations that interest students.
2. The extent to which science is studied and understood is increased, with a significant economy of time, when mathematics and science are integrated.
3. There is improved quality of learning and retention, supporting the thesis that learning which is meaningful and relevant is more effective.
4. Motivation and involvement are increased dramatically as students investigate real world situations and participate actively in the process.

We invite you to become part of this classroom teacher movement by using an integrated approach to learning and sharing any suggestions you may have. The AIMS Program welcomes you!

AIMS Education Foundation Programs

A Day With AIMS

Intensive one-day workshops are offered to introduce educators to the philosophy and rationale of AIMS. Participants will discuss the methodology of AIMS and the strategies by which AIMS principles may be incorporated into curriculum. Each participant will take part in a variety of hands-on AIMS investigations to gain an understanding of such aspects as the scientific/mathematical content, classroom management, and connections with other curricular areas. The *A Day With AIMS* workshops may be offered anywhere in the United States. Necessary supplies and take-home materials are usually included in the enrollment fee.

AIMS One-Week Off-Campus Workshops

Throughout the nation, AIMS offers many one-week workshops each year, usually in the summer. Each workshop lasts five days and includes at least 30 hours of AIMS hands-on instruction. Participants are grouped according to the grade level(s) in which they are interested. Instructors are members of the AIMS National Leadership Network. Supplies for the activities and a generous supply of take-home materials are included in the enrollment fee. Sites are selected on the basis of applications submitted by educational organizations. If chosen to host a workshop, the host agency agrees to provide specified facilities and cooperate in the promotion of the workshop. The AIMS Education Foundation supplies workshop materials as well as the travel, housing, and meals for instructors.

AIMS One-Week On-Campus Workshops

Each summer, Fresno Pacific College offers AIMS one-week workshops on the campus of Fresno Pacific College in Fresno, California. AIMS Program Directors and highly qualified members of the AIMS National Leadership Network serve as instructors.

The Science Festival and the Festival of Mathematics

Each summer, Fresno Pacific College offers a Science Festival and a Festival of Mathematics. These two-week festivals have gained national recognition as inspiring and challenging experiences, giving unique opportunities to experience hands-on mathematics and science in topical and grade level groups. Guest faculty includes some of the nation's most highly regarded mathematics and science educators. Supplies and take-home materials are included in the enrollment fee.

The AIMS National Leadership Program

This is an AIMS staff development program seeking to prepare facilitators for a leadership roles in science/math education in their home districts or regions. Upon successful completion of the program, trained facilitators become members of the AIMS National Leadership Network, qualified to conduct AIMS workshops, teach AIMS in-service courses for college credit, and serve as AIMS consultants. Intensive training is provided in mathematics, science, processing skills, workshop management, and other relevant topics.

College Credit and Grants

Those who participate in workshops may often qualify for college credit. If the workshop takes place on the campus of Fresno Pacific College, that institution may grant appropriate credit. If the workshop takes place off-campus, arrangements can sometimes be made for credit to be granted by another college or university. In addition, the applicant's home school district is often willing to grant in-service or professional development credit. Many educators who participate in AIMS workshops are recipients of various types of educational grants, either local or national. Nationally known foundations and funding agencies have long recognized the value of AIMS mathematics and science workshops to educators. The AIMS Education Foundation encourages educators interested in attending or hosting workshops to explore the possibilities suggested above. Although the Foundation strongly supports such interest, it reminds applicants that they have the primary responsibility for fulfilling *current* requirements.

For current information regarding the programs described above, please complete the following:

Information Request

Please send current information on the items checked:

____ *Basic Information Packet* on AIMS materials
____ *Festival of Mathematics*
____ *Science Festival*
____ *AIMS National Leadership Program*

____ *AIMS One-Week On-Campus Workshops*
____ *AIMS One-Week Off-Campus Workshops*
____ Hosting information for *A Day With AIMS* workshops
____ Hosting information for *A Week With AIMS* workshops

Name _____

Address _____
        Street   City   State   Zip

Mail to **AIMS Education Foundation**, P.O. Box 8120, Fresno, CA 93747-8120

AIMS Program Publications

GRADES 5-9 SERIES

Math + Science, A Solution
The Sky's the Limit
From Head to Toe
Fun With Foods
Floaters and Sinkers
Down to Earth
Our Wonderful World
Pieces and Patterns, A Patchwork in Math and Science
Piezas y Diseños, un Mosaic de Matemáticas y Ciencias
Out of This World
Soap Films and Bubbles
Finding Your Bearings
Electrical Connections
Historical Connections in Mathematics
Machine Shop

GRADES K-4 SERIES

Fall Into Math and Science
Cáete de Gusto Hacia el Otoño con la Matemáticas y Ciencias
Glide Into Winter With Math and Science
Patine al Invierno con Matemáticas y Ciencias
Spring Into Math and Science
Brinca de Alegria Hacia la Primavera con las Matemáticas y Ciencias
Seasoning Math and Science, Book A (Fall and Winter)
Seasoning Math and Science, Book B (Spring and Summer)
Jawbreakers and Heart Thumpers
Hardhatting in a Geo-World
Popping With Power
Overhead and Underfoot
Primarily Plants
Primariamente Plantas
Primarily Physics
Primariamente Física

GRADES K-6 SERIES

Primarily Bears
Ositos Nada Más
Water Precious Water
Critters
Mostly Magnets

FOR FURTHER INFORMATION WRITE TO:
AIMS Education Foundation • P.O. Box 8120 • Fresno, California 93747-8120

We invite you to subscribe to *AIMS!*

Each issue of *AIMS* contains a variety of material useful to educators at all grade levels. Feature articles of lasting value deal with topics such as mathematical or science concepts, curriculum, assessment, the teaching of processing skills, and historical background. Several of the latest AIMS math/science investigations are always included, along with their reproducible activity sheets. As needs direct and space allows, various issues contain news of current developments, such as workshop schedules, activities of the AIMS National Leadership Network, and announcements of upcoming publications.

AIMS is published monthly, August through May. Subscriptions are on an annual basis only. A subscription entered at any time will begin with the next issue, but will also include the previous issues of that volume. Readers have preferred this arrangement because articles and activities within an annual volume are often interrelated.

Please note that an *AIMS* subscription automatically includes duplication rights for one school site for all issues included in the subscription. Many schools build cost-effective library resources with their subscriptions.

YES! I am interested in subscribing to *AIMS*.

Name _____   Home Phone _____

Address _____   City, State Zip _____

Please send the following volumes (subject to availability):

_____	Volume I (1986-87)	$22.50
_____	Volume II (1987-88)	$22.50
_____	Volume III (1988-89)	$22.50
_____	Volume IV (1989-90)	$22.50
_____	Volume V (1990-91)	$22.50
_____	Volume VI (1991-92)	$25.00
_____	Volume VII (1992-93)	$25.00
_____	Volume VIII (1993-94)	$25.00
_____	Limited offer: Volumes VIII & IX (1993-94 & 1994-95) $45.00	

(Note: Prices may change without notice. For current prices, call (209) 255-4094.)

Check your method of payment:

☐ Check enclosed in the amount of
☐ Purchase order attached (Please be sure it includes the P.O. number, the authorizing signature, and the position of the authorizing person.)
☐ Credit Card (Check One)
   ☐ Visa   ☐ MasterCard   Number _____

Amount $ _____   Expiration Date _____

Signature _____   Today's Date _____

Make checks payable to **AIMS Education Foundation.**
Mail to *AIMS Magazine*, P.O. Box 8120, Fresno, CA 93747-8120.

AIMS Duplication Rights Program

AIMS has received many requests from school districts for the purchase of unlimited duplication rights to AIMS materials. In response, the AIMS Education Foundation has formulated the program outlined below. There is a built-in flexibility which, we trust, will provide for those who use AIMS materials extensively to purchase such rights for either individual activities or entire books.

It is the goal of the AIMS Education Foundation to make its materials and programs available at reasonable cost. All income from sale of publications and duplication rights is used to support AIMS programs. Hence, strict adherence to regulations governing duplication is essential. Duplication of AIMS materials beyond limits set by copyright laws and those specified below is strictly forbidden.

Limited Duplication Rights

Any purchaser of an AIMS book may make up to *200 copies* of any activity in that book for use at *one school site*. Beyond that, rights must be purchased according to the appropriate category.

Unlimited Duplication Rights for Single Activities

An individual or school may purchase the right to make an unlimited number of copies of a single activity. The royalty is $5.00 per activity per school site.

Examples: 3 activities x 1 site x $5.00 = $15.00
           9 activities x 3 sites x $5.00 = $135.00

Unlimited Duplication Rights for Whole Books

A school or district may purchase the right to make an unlimited number of copies of a single, *specified* book. The royalty is $20.00 per book per school site. This is in addition to the cost of the book.

Examples: 5 books x 1 site x $20.00 = $100.00
          12 books x 10 sites x $20.00 = $2400.00

Newsletter Duplication Rights

Members of the AIMS Education Foundation who receive the AIMS Newsletter may make an unlimited number of copies of activities for use only at the member's school site. School districts must join separately for each school desiring to duplicate activities.

Workshop Instructors' Duplication Rights

Workshop instructors may distribute to registered workshop participants: a maximum of 100 copies of any article and /or 100 copies of no more than 8 activities, provided these 6 conditions are met:

1. Since all AIMS activities are based upon the AIMS Model of Mathematics and the AIMS Model of Learning, leaders must include in their presentations an explanation of these two models.
2. Workshop instructors must relate the AIMS activities presented to these basic explanations of the AIMS philosophy of education.
3. The copyright notice must appear on all materials distributed.
4. Instructors must provide information enabling participants to apply for membership in the AIMS Education Foundation or order books from the Foundation.
5. Instructors must inform participants of their limited duplication rights as outlined below.
6. Only student pages may be duplicated.

Written permission must be obtained for duplication beyond the limits listed above. Additional royalty payments may be required.

Workshop Participants' Rights

Those enrolled in workshops in which AIMS student activity sheets are distributed may duplicate a maximum of 35 copies or enough to use the lessons one time with one class, whichever is less. Beyond that, rights must be purchased according to the appropriate category.

Application for Duplication Rights

The purchasing agency or individual must clearly specify the following:
1. Name, address, and telephone number
2. Titles of the books for Unlimited Duplication Rights contracts
3. Titles of activities for Unlimited Duplication Rights contracts
4. Names and addresses of school sites for which duplication rights are being purchased

NOTE: Books to be duplicated must be purchased separately and are not included in the contract for Unlimited Duplication Rights.

The requested duplication rights are automatically authorized when proper payment is received, although a *Certificate of Duplication Rights* will be issued when the application is processed.

Address all correspondence to

> **Contract Division**
> **AIMS Education Foundation**
> **P.O. Box 8120**
> **Fresno, CA 93747-8120**